Greg Taylor is the editor of the online alternative news portal, "The Daily Grail" (www.dailygrail.com), and is also the editor-in-chief of *Sub Rosa Magazine*. Greg has a long history of research into the subjects of alternative history and secret societies. He lives in Australia with his wife and two children.

www.dailygrail.com

THE GUIDE TO
DAN BROWN'S
THE SOLOMON KEY

GREG TAYLOR

DEVORSS & COMPANY
CAMARILLO, CALIFORNIA

The Guide to Dan Brown's The Solomon Key
© Greg Taylor 2005

ISBN: 0875168167
Library of Congress Control Number: 2005929752

FIRST DEVORSS EDITION, 2005

Cover art by Mark James Foster
http://www.artifice-design.co.uk/

Masonic Cipher and Symbols Font
© 5999 A.L., ODR Lodge #188, F&AM of California
http://www.ODR.org/

DeVorss & Company, Publisher
P.O. Box 1389
Camarillo CA 93011-1389
www.devorss.com

Printed in the United States of America

CONTENTS

FOR DAD...

ACKNOWLEDGEMENTS

The occasion of releasing your first book is one which truly makes you appreciate the help you have received along the way. It would certainly be impossible to list all those who have positively influenced me during my journey, but the following deserve special mention.

To all of the authors and researchers who have contributed to the TDG project, many thanks. Special mention to Rudolf Gantenbrink, Robert Bauval, Graham Hancock, Robert Lomas, Ralph Ellis, Lynn Picknett, Clive Prince, Filip Coppens, Alan Boyle, Steven Mizrach, Marcus Williamson, Doug Kenyon, Chip Meyers, Steve Nixon, Ian Lawton, and Chris Ogilvie-Herald. Also to all the TDG community for their continuing support, and a tip of the hat to Jim Alison for graciously sharing his images with me.

Thanks also to Mitch Horowitz for his invaluable advice and generous spirit, and Frater Ijynx and his percussionist friend for their magick and music. Much respect to Bill Block at Key Creatives, and my Italian agents Asni, Ranghetti and Rotundo for their belief in this book and dedication to 'getting it out there'.

To the engine room of the Daily Grail: Bill Bellamy, James Kennedy, Steve Hynd, Rick Gned, Kat Lowry and the gone-but-not-forgotten Rich Shelton. Your good humour, intelligence, and unfathomable tolerance of hard work for little reward is largely responsible for the success of the site. I can only wonder at the good fortune that has directed me to become associated with each of you.

To Simon Cox, for sharing ideas and plotting the overthrow of the paradigm with me. And to Mark Foster, whose artistic genius only pales beside his good heart.

To the Binya crew, for being soul-brothers. Special thanks to David Pickworth for his willingness to help me out regardless of time or effort involved, and for being one of the most sincere human beings on the planet. You rock Doppel.

Lastly, to my family. The last few years have been a hard time for us all, but I think it has shown the true heart of our clan. To Dad, Mum, Leanne, Nat, Scott and Keith – thanks for everything. To Tony, Narelle, Mark and Lee, thank you for accepting me unconditionally. Most special love and thanks to Tonita, for sharing her life and love with me. My life was blessed the day we met, I love you sweetheart. And to Isis and Phoenix, who make the sun rise each day for me, I give my unconditional love.

NOTHING BUT THE KEY IS WANTING

When Dan Brown released his novel *The Da Vinci Code* in 2003, he would have been hoping for some success. In 1996 Brown had taken the biggest gamble of his life, giving up his job as an English teacher at the prestigious Phillips Exeter Academy in order to write fiction novels for a living. His first novel, *Digital Fortress*, explored the controversial debate between national security interests versus civilian privacy, through the medium of one of Brown's favourite hobbies: cryptography. However, despite becoming a #1 national bestselling e-Book, *Digital Fortress* only sold moderately well in bookstores.

Two follow-up novels, *Deception Point* and *Angels and Demons*, met with similar receptions, although with the latter Brown hit upon a potent recipe that would carry his next work to great success. In *Angels and Demons* we meet for the first time the now famous character of Robert Langdon, a Harvard Professor of Religious Symbology called in by authorities to help solve mysterious crimes, on account of his comprehensive knowledge of symbols and codes.

Just as *Digital Fortress* juxtaposed national security with civilian privacy, the plot of *Angels and Demons* was based around the dichotomy of science and religion – perhaps a reflection of Brown's own influences, growing up as the son of a Presidential Award-winning math professor and a professional sacred musician. The storyline, which involved an ancient secret society engaged in a centuries-old battle with the Catholic Church, allowed the author to include a number of interesting, though disparate, topics: cutting-edge science, conspiracy theories, religious symbolism and cryptography.

The 'treasure hunt' aspect is a key ingredient in Dan Brown's novels, and is based on his own love of cryptography. During his childhood, his mathematician father would create treasure hunts for his children involving ciphers and codes. Brown would later insert this little bit of personal history into the character of Sophie Neveu in *The Da Vinci Code*. The appeal to the reader is obvious: the cryptographic codes and symbolism draw the reader in on a personal level as they try to solve each problem, while the aspects of 'hidden history' reward through a sense of revelation, the unveiling of secrets. John Chadwick, the philologist and cryptanalyst who helped decipher the early Greek language script 'Linear B', aptly described the human affinity for secrets and puzzles in his book *The Decipherment of Linear B*:

> *The urge to discover secrets is deeply ingrained in human nature; even the least curious mind is roused by the promise of sharing knowledge withheld from others...most of us are driven to sublimate this urge by the solving of artificial puzzles devised for our entertainment.*[1]

Dan Brown's melding of the detective-thriller genre with the subject of secret societies and alternative histories proved to be an inspirational combination in his next novel *The Da Vinci Code*. Referencing the historical mystery of the secret society known as the Priory of Sion, and embedding legends of art history within his cryptographic puzzles, Brown finally realized his dreams of writing a best-seller – on a massive scale.

Rarely has a novel set such benchmarks. Since its release in 2003, *The Da Vinci Code* has broken sales records all over the globe. As of March 2005, there were more than 25 million copies of the book in print. As a bonus, the success of the book has meant that Brown's earlier novels are now all best-sellers as well. Amazingly, in early 2004 all four of Brown's novels held places on the *New York Times* bestseller list during the same week – an incredible accomplishment. Not to mention, Columbia Pictures has now bought the movie rights to the novel, with Oscar-winners Ron Howard signing on to direct the film version, and Tom Hanks playing Robert Langdon.

The Da Vinci Code has also had a huge sociological influence. Dan Brown's use of heretical themes, such as the marriage of Jesus to Mary Magdalene, has led to widespread controversy and much discussion over the 'true history' of Christianity – and in particular, Catholicism. In March 2005, the Vatican reacted by going on the offensive against Brown's bestseller: in an unprecedented attack on a fictional book, Cardinal Tarcisio Bertone, the Archbishop of Genoa, accused the novel of being "filled with lies and manipulations." Cardinal Bertone described Dan Brown's heretical plotline as "deplorable", and urged Catholic bookstores to take the thriller off their shelves.

THE SOLOMON KEY COMETH

However, it's worth asking if Dan Brown was just hoping for success, or whether he was in fact planning on it. The initial release of *The Da Vinci Code* was accompanied by the publishing equivalent of a frontal assault. Brown's publisher Doubleday initially sent out some 10,000 free copies of the book to influential reviewers and major bookshops, quite a substantial risk investment as Brown was – at that time – an only moderately successful author. In fact, the number of free copies sent out was around half the number that Brown's previous three novels had sold altogether. The bold move paid off however, with early reviews generating a word-of-mouth campaign which would guarantee profound success for the novel.

Additionally, it is now obvious that Dan Brown planned *The Da Vinci Code* to be the first in a series of books that would be marketed together, for on the dust jacket of the U.S. edition of *The Da Vinci Code* can be found a number of ciphers which reference the subject matter of Brown's *next* book. When originally found by readers, the coded messages were ambiguous and confusing to say the least. However, the reason for their inclusion became obvious when Dan Brown announced in an interview that clues about his next novel could be found on the dust jacket of *The Da Vinci Code*. Soon after, Brown's official website announced a competition titled "Uncover the Code: The Secret is Hidden Right Before Your Eyes."

With the enticement of a trip to Paris for the winner, the Internet challenge began with these words:

Welcome fellow reader of The Da Vinci Code.

Leonardo was a known trickster who liked to hide secrets in plain sight...often encoded within his artwork. Now, like the secrets hidden in Leonardo's art, a series of codes has been hidden for you.

Disguised on the jacket of The Da Vinci Code, numerous encrypted messages hint at the subject matter of Dan Brown's next Robert Langdon novel. [2]

The inclusion of the codes on the book jacket was a masterstroke on the part of Brown and his publisher, and one which showed admirable foresight. Hundreds of thousands of fans have since participated in the competition on Brown's website, and Internet forums have long threads discussing the solutions. Building on the air of expectation by slowly revealing hints about the next book, Brown has managed to generate an almost hysterical level of anticipation. So much so that when Brown's publisher Stephen Rubin let slip the title of the coming novel, it was enough to warrant a story in the *New York Times*.[3]

In case you haven't heard yet, the title of the next book will be *The Solomon Key*, and it is tentatively scheduled to appear in early 2006.

RIDDLE ME THIS

This book is written in the spirit of Dan Brown's approach to writing and marketing. Firstly, we'll take a look at his comments in the media and on his website to look for subtle clues as to the likely topics in his next book. Then we'll solidify some of those thoughts by investigating the codes left by Brown on the cover of *The Da Vinci Code* and in the related Internet challenge, and interpret their meaning. Lastly, we'll study the *personal symbology* of Dan Brown – his writing style and historical influences

– and attempt to predict possible storylines and plot devices in *The Solomon Key*, before the book is even on the shelves.

Once we have this clear grounding in Dan Brown's influences and topics of choice, we'll follow it up with a more detailed investigation of the subjects we've uncovered. And while it's obvious that we can't predict every detail – and no doubt some of our predictions will be plain wrong – you can be sure that much of what we uncover in our investigation will play a part in *The Solomon Key*.

Let's get started...

CHAPTER 1

THE RAW DATA

L et's begin with a study of Dan Brown's own words on the sequel to *The Da Vinci Code*. Initially, we have little need to delve into predictions and guesswork in order to surmise the main topic of *The Solomon Key*, as the "Frequently Asked Questions" area on Dan Brown's website gives us the answer. In response to a query regarding his fascination with secret societies, Brown answers with these words:

> *My interest sparks from growing up in New England, surrounded by the clandestine clubs of Ivy League universities, the Masonic lodges of our Founding Fathers, and the hidden hallways of early government power...the next Robert Langdon novel...is set deep within the oldest fraternity in history...the enigmatic brotherhood of the Masons.*[4]

In this passage we have initial confirmation that *The Solomon Key* will involve Freemasonry, a secret society which is vaguely familiar to most, if only by name – superficially thought of by those not completely familiar with it as either as a quaint but innocent 'old boys' network, or alternately as a Machiavellian machine of subversive power. A mass of contradictory literature is available on Masonry, and it's often difficult to figure out where the legends end and truth begins when it comes to the history of this enigmatic group. Dan Brown will no doubt draw on many of the more conspiratorial elements of the history of Masonry, but what sources will he use for *The Solomon Key*? We'll delve more deeply into this topic a little later.

Interestingly, Brown also makes casual reference in the passage to a number of other related topics – the Masonic lodges of the 'Founding Fathers', the 'hidden hallways' of power, and the secret fraternities of the Ivy League universities. While not stating explicitly that these topics are part of his new book, the mention of three such closely related topics deserves our attention.

It is a well-known fact that a number of the Founding Fathers of the United States were Freemasons. George Washington, Benjamin Franklin and Paul Revere are all known to have been initiated into Masonry. There are a variety of 'hidden history' theories which posit that the founding of America was a Masonic project to build a Utopian land, free of the errors of the 'old world', and that this 'conspiracy' continues to this day. Supporters of these theories point to a number of pieces of evidence, not least the planning and architecture of the U.S capital, Washington, D.C., and strange symbolism implanted within the Great Seal of the United States. They also bring our attention to the list of Presidents who have been Freemasons, and the current prominence of the Ivy League secret society, Skull and Bones.

Could it be that Dan Brown will be basing *The Solomon Key* on some of these hidden histories? It seems we may have stumbled on another piece of the puzzle, because in an interview with Ruth Mariampolski, Brown was quoted as saying:

*Currently I'm writing another Robert Langdon thriller – the
sequel to The Da Vinci Code. For the first time, Langdon will
find himself embroiled in a mystery on U.S. soil. This new
novel explores the hidden history of our nation's capital.*

It's also worth noting that Dan Brown is completely
familiar with the bizarre iconography present in the Great
Seal of the United States, as it was mentioned in his first
Robert Langdon novel, *Angels and Demons*. When asked what
he thought these symbols had to do with the United States,
Brown answered...

> *...absolutely nothing, which is what makes their presence
> on our currency so remarkable...the eye inside the triangle
> is a pagan symbol adopted by the Illuminati to signify the
> brotherhood's ability to infiltrate and watch all things.* [5]

Not to mention, the 'eye within the triangle' motif is actually
present on the cover of *The Da Vinci Code* – although we'll save
the analysis of that for a later section. Hence, if Dan Brown does
incorporate the imagery of the Great Seal into *The Solomon Key*,
we should expect it to be related to the Illuminati, or at least an
organization closely allied to it.

We have so far picked up some strong clues as to the main
themes likely for *The Solomon Key*. Before we move on to an
investigation of the enigmatic ciphers left on the cover of *The Da
Vinci Code,* and the related Internet puzzle, we should quickly
mention one more hint left by Dan Brown. Remarking on how
Robert Langdon discusses Kabbalistic numerology in *The Da
Vinci Code*, Brown relates that...

> *...the book also drops a hint as to the identity of another
> ultrasecret numerology sect that fascinates me, but I can't*

*reveal their name here without ruining much of the surprise
of the next book.*

No obvious answer to this clue comes to mind here – a survey
of historical sects interested in numerology would certainly turn
up a long list. So we'll just store that one for now, and move on
to the "Da Vinci Challenge".

RIGHT BEFORE YOUR EYES

As we mentioned in the Introduction, the dust jacket of
the U.S. edition of *The Da Vinci Code* contains a number of
ciphers which reference the subject matter of *The Solomon
Key.* An Internet competition was announced, ending in April
2004, which illuminated some of these confusing codes, by
asking questions in relation to them. We'll now work through
both the questions and answers in an attempt to discover more
about Brown's upcoming book.

The first three questions of the challenge are more a test
that you have read *The Da Vinci Code,* and are easily answered
giving way to the challenge proper. The first real question
asks the reader to look on the back cover of *The Da Vinci
Code,* and search for a coded reference written backwards.
Keen observation – and a mirror – reveals a mysterious map
reference: 37º 57' 6.5" North and 77º 8' 44" West. Before the
Internet challenge was made available, those who had found
this code struck a dead end when they looked up the location.
Why this was so became clear once the related question was
asked on the website:

*Q1. What enigmatic sculpture stands one degree North of
the location indicated in the code?*

Adding on a degree to the latitude made more sense, as it pointed at the headquarters of the Central Intelligence Agency (C.I.A.) in Langley, Virginia. Most people interested in cryptography are very familiar with the "enigmatic sculpture" which resides there, as it is ranked as one of the top unsolved puzzles in the world today.

A1. Kryptos.

Located in the courtyard and surroundings of C.I.A. headquarters in Langley is a sculpture named "Kryptos". Created by American artist James Sanborn, Kryptos is actually a number of sculptures, although the most recognized piece is a large vertical "S" shaped screen inscribed with 865 characters,

Kryptos Sculpture, Langley

in which four separate messages are encoded, each with its own cipher. Sanborn has revealed that there is an additional riddle which will be solvable only after the four encrypted passages have been decrypted. Since its dedication in 1990, three of the four codes have been cracked, while the fourth remains unsolved.

Apparently Dan Brown, a self-confessed cryptography nut, has long been interested in the Kryptos story. In fact, rumors suggest that he is working closely with Sanborn as part of *The Solomon Key*[6]. Interestingly, early reports said that Kryptos had been designed in collaboration with a "prominent fiction writer." While this was well before Dan Brown's time, and Sanborn has since disputed the claim, does it indicate a facet of the creation of Kryptos which Dan Brown may have been able to 'buy into'? As an aside, in a TV interview, when asked about the sculpture, Brown replied that it "refers to the ancient mysteries". We will discuss the Kryptos enigma in more detail later.

Once "Kryptos" is entered as the answer on the website challenge, we are taken to a new page which gives a little background information on Sanborn's Kryptos sculpture, and refers to one of the cracked codes (the second). The deciphered message reads:

> *They used the earth's magnetic field. The information was gathered and transmitted underground to an unknown location. Does Langley know about this? They should: it's buried out there somewhere. Who knows the exact location?*

The website then asks for the concluding part of this text.

> *Q2. According to Kryptos, what are the initials of the person who "knows the exact location?"*

The answer to this question is reasonably simple, once you are familiar with the Kryptos story. The final phrase in the deciphered message from Kryptos is "Only WW knows":

A2. WW

The website challenge offers no further comment on this answer. Most people have assumed that the 'WW' referred to is the C.I.A. director at the time of the sculpture's dedication, William Webster. The C.I.A., no doubt wary of an embarrassing message being encoded by the artist, had insisted that Sanborn give Webster an envelope containing the code and the message. Thus, WW should certainly know the solution. Others have cautioned against such an easy answer, and continue to search for other options – some people have even pointed out that WW turned upside down is MM, the initials of Mary Magdalene. In any case, the phrase "only WW knows" can also be found discretely hidden upside down on the back cover of *The Da Vinci Code*.

The next question in the challenge changes the topic, and the question following it references the answer. It directs readers to look on the cover flap for a coded message:

Q3. Within those paragraphs (and shrouded fast), resides a mystic phrase from ages past. To make your quest…abandon any fears, if you are bold the font of truth appears.

The message is easily deciphered by picking out the bolded letters from the rest of the text. It reveals a phrase which will be worth plenty of discussion:

A3. Is there no help for the widow's son.

The website then asks a fourth question based on this phrase, and it makes perfect sense in light of the opening to our chapter:

> *Q4. For which ancient brotherhood (still active today) does this phrase have special meaning?*

The "widow's son" is a well-known term in Freemasonry, and the whole phrase "is there no help for the widow's son" is actually a coded call for assistance used by the brethren when facing danger. Some researchers have suggested that the "widow's son" phrase could be a code for the son of Jesus and Mary Magdalene – a pertinent idea considering the theme of *The Da Vinci Code*. There is also another possible significance to this phrase…but that topic will have to wait as we are almost at the end of the web challenge. Let's fill in the answer for the fourth clue:

> *A4. Freemasons*

If we didn't already have enough confirmation that the mysterious fraternal organization would feature in *The Solomon Key*, we can certainly take this at face value. The website challenge offers some comment on the answer, describing Freemasonry as one of the oldest fraternities in existence, a "system of morality, veiled in allegory, and illustrated by symbols." What more natural choice of topic for a Robert Langdon thriller could there be? In early 2005, final confirmation of this fact emerged with publicity for the book stating that the plot "is built around the murders of several current political leaders by someone with ties to the Freemasons, the secretive fraternity that included some of the Founding Fathers."

The final question of the challenge is far more cryptic, and requires both a keen eye and a little cryptographic knowledge (or intuition). The clue given points to a very faint seal on the back cover of *The Da Vinci Code,* in which a series of numbers are given, separated by the 'eye in the triangle' symbol. The clue then describes how to solve the riddle:

> *Each number to a chapter points the way*
> *Each chapter starts with words in muted gray*
> *The letter that is first is what you seek*
> *Thirteen of them (and though it all looks Greek)*
> *Add three all-seeing-eyes – a perfect square*
> *Begin at E, and Caesar guides you there.*

The directions end with the question:

> *Q5. What famous phrase is printed around the seal?*

Using the numbers and cross-checking with each chapter we gather thirteen letters, which don't make a whole lot of sense in their current order. Thirteen letters and three all-seeing-eyes add up to sixteen characters in all, a perfect four by four square just as the clue says. But how do we form this square using the letters and eyes? The clue leads the way – "Caesar guides you there". While a number of cipher techniques were used by Julius Caesar, one in particular suits the use of a square, the so-called 'Caesar Box'. To employ a Caesar Box, the cipher text is laid out in vertical columns within the square, and then the coded message is revealed by reading across horizontally via the rows. Using this method, and taking the all-seeing eyes as 'spaces' between the words, an intriguing phrase is unveiled:

A5. E Pluribus Unum

After entering the answer, the challenge explains the phrase. It describes how "E Pluribus Unum" is Latin for "Out of Many...One", and that it appears on the Great Seal of the United States. It also notes that these motifs can be found on the dollar bill, adding that discussion of the various theories involved will have to wait for another day. We'll beat Dan Brown to the punch and do exactly that a little later, when we devote a whole section to the Great Seal and its appearance on the currency of the United States.

By answering the five questions correctly, we are taken to a final page which consists of one last challenge. It says that to complete the quest, we are required to click on the "oeil droit" of the Mona Lisa. This is a simple enough task, as "oeil droit" is French for "right eye". Clicking on the right eye of the Mona Lisa completes the challenge. However, perhaps we should note the choice of the right eye as a further clue to the content of *The Solomon Key*?

Dan Brown regularly reminds us in *The Da Vinci Code,* on his website, and in interviews that many of 'the mysteries' in his novels are based on the idea of a continuation of hidden knowledge from ancient times. One of the ancient traditions from which he draws on regularly for his 'symbology' is that of the great Egyptian culture which existed for some 3,000 years before the time of Christianity. And the 'right eye' held a certain meaning for the ancient Egyptians.

The 'udjat', or 'Eye of Horus', was a particularly potent symbol to the Ancient Egyptians. Examples of this motif can be found on temple walls and inscribed on pyramidions, but it was most often used as an amulet worn by the living or included in the mummy wrappings of the deceased. It has a curious mythological origin: the god Horus is said to have lost his eye during a battle with rival god Seth, the murderer of his father Osiris (interestingly, this makes Horus a "widow's son" as well, the widow in question being the goddess Isis):

Seth tore the eye into pieces. Thoth...was able to reassemble them...Thoth gave the Eye to Horus. Horus, in turn, gave the eye to his murdered father Osiris, thereby bringing him back to life.[7]

The symbol was most often depicted anatomically as the right eye, although both left and right held their own meaning. The right eye of Horus, also termed the 'Eye of Ra', was consonant with the Sun – and on Hermetic grounds has therefore been associated with masculinity, rationality and science. The left eye was associated with the Moon – and was therefore ascribed femininity, intuition, and esoteric thought according to Hermetic philosophy. Interestingly, Masonic iconography often portrays both the Sun and the Moon together in the one image.

As an amulet, the Eye of Horus was believed to have healing and protective power, even the ability to resurrect the dead (as was the case with Osiris). The icon was also used as a mathematical device, with the different 'shreds' of the torn-up eye each

Eye of Horus 'Udjat' Amulet (© Jon Bodsworth)

representing a fraction of the whole. Could Dan Brown use this bit of trivia in one of his codes? Perhaps more pertinently, the Eye of Horus is also thought by some to have served as the model for the all-seeing-eye commonly associated with secret societies including the Illuminati and the Freemasons, and mentioned previously by Brown. This may be based on the function of the eye, which is to perceive light, an allusion to the spiritual ability to see the 'inner light'.

However, we should also keep in mind this division of the two eyes of Horus as signifying the rational and intuitive sides of human consciousness. As we mentioned in the Introduction, Dan Brown's storylines often revolve around similar dichotomies to these. In *Angels and Demons*, the battle between the Illuminati and the Catholic Church was described as a battle between science and religion. Ironically, in *The Da Vinci Code*, the Church was depicted as the domination of the masculine, and the Priory of Sion the defender of the 'sacred feminine'. With the secret societies in each case being depicted at the opposite ends of the Hermetic spectrum, it may be difficult to decide where Dan Brown will position Freemasonry in *The Solomon Key*. Further investigation may illuminate the issue though (no pun intended), so we'll mark that down as another subject to discuss in more depth.

THE SYMBOLOGY OF DAN BROWN

What can we glean from Dan Brown's previous novels, in terms of research and writing, that may aid us in piecing together *The Solomon Key*? Quite a lot actually, as there are a number of consistent themes which recur in his work which should give us a broad idea of the subjects which will be in the next book. Also, by comparing his normal plot devices to the possibilities allowed by the subject matter of the new book, we may well be able to predict a few of the minor details of *The Solomon Key*. What are the similar themes of Dan Brown's two Robert Langdon novels? Where do we start? Wikipedia, the free online encyclopedia, lists these similarities between the plots[8]:

- The main character, Robert Langdon, follows a trail of mystical, ancient clues involving a secret society and its opposition to the Catholic Church.

- Each novel begins with a prologue involving an assassin, and a murder scene with strange symbols. Each time Langdon is woken by a telephone call requesting his assistance in solving the case.

- The plots of both novels take place over the course of just one day, and see Langdon teamed with a beautiful, intelligent woman who is closely related to the murder victim.

- The assassin in each book (the Hassassin in *Angels and Demons* and Silas in *The Da Vinci Code*) is under the impression that he is acting on behalf of an organization, which is in fact being framed for the murders (the Illuminati and Opus Dei respectively).

- The mastermind behind the murders in each book turns out to be a character who would be expected to have the least motive for doing so.

- Langdon and the female lead end the story romantically (and perhaps sexually) involved.

While the criticism leveled at Brown for such similar plots may inspire him to change tack from this formula, we can nevertheless still expect a number of elements of his style to reappear, as they are so closely linked with his success.

Hidden History:

Dan Brown's novels involving Robert Langdon have both drawn on alternative history sources. *The Da Vinci Code* relied heavily on the mythos surrounding the Priory of Sion, a secret society claiming ancestry back to the time of the Crusades. The pedigree of the Priory of Sion was tentatively established in 1981 in the best-selling alternative history book *Holy Blood, Holy Grail*. We know for a fact that Dan Brown holds this book in high regard, as he gave it the honor of gracing Leigh Teabing's bookshelf in *The Da Vinci Code*. In fact, Teabing singles it out as "perhaps the best-known tome" on the topic of the bloodline of Jesus. The attentive reader may even pick out a little in-joke left by Brown: "Leigh Teabing" is an anagram constructed from the surnames of two of the co-authors of *Holy Blood, Holy Grail* – Richard Leigh and Michael Baigent (the other author involved being Henry Lincoln).

We might query why Henry Lincoln's name was omitted from the anagram. Perhaps it was simply for ease of creating a believable name for Teabing? There may be another reason though. After the publication of *Holy Blood, Holy Grail* and its 'sequel' *The Messianic Legacy*, Baigent and Leigh went on to author more books together – without Lincoln. One of these books is specifically concerned with the history of Freemasonry. *The Temple and the Lodge*, released in 1989, traces the possible links between the dissolution of the legendary Knights Templar and the beginnings of Freemasonry. As part of their investigation they found significant links between Freemasonry and Rosslyn

Chapel, an historic landmark that readers of *The Da Vinci Code* will find immediately familiar. Beyond that though, the ending of *The Temple and the Lodge* provides a clue to our own quest, as it deals with the Masonic influences involved in the formation of the United States of America. Is Dan a fan of the duo?

Another book on Teabing's bookshelf is *The Templar Revelation*, by Lynn Picknett and Clive Prince. This book also argues for an unbroken lineage between the Knights Templar, citing both *The Temple and the Lodge* as well as another book, *Born in Blood* by John Robinson. It also is one of the key 'alternative history' books to promote the idea of a 'cult of the sacred feminine'.

The section of *The Da Vinci Code* relating to Rosslyn Chapel certainly drew partly upon the two books mentioned above, but it would appear that there was at least one other work referenced. When Robert and Sophie get to this curious landmark, Brown describes it as having been designed by the Knights Templar as an exact architectural blueprint of the original Solomon's Temple in Jerusalem. There is also mention of a 'Seal of Solomon' marked in the Chapel by key architectural points. Both of these ideas were first put forward in a book called *The Hiram Key* (note the similarity to Brown's next title), by authors Robert Lomas and Christopher Knight. Interestingly, both Knight and Lomas are Freemasons, and a number of their books delve into the history of their own order and uncover strange facts and correspondences outside of orthodox history. We should therefore pay close attention to their writings.

Why does Dan Brown base the plots of his novels on these often controversial books? Probably because 'alternative history' books offer the reader the thrill of subversive revelation: the "they didn't teach this in school" factor. The 'secret society' edge to these histories also adds much intrigue to the storyline, and offers up any number of possible plots. In *Angels and Demons*,

Brown introduces the 'Illuminati' as a shadowy organization moving beneath the radar of orthodox history. In *The Da Vinci Code* this role is played by the Priory of Sion. In *The Solomon Key* it looks likely that Freemasonry, or at least some part of the brotherhood, will be used in a similar way.

So what other 'alternative history' books might be worth looking at, in light of what we have discovered so far about *The Solomon Key*? If it involves the 'secret history' of Washington, D.C., then we should perhaps take note of the book *The Secret Architecture of Our Nation's Capital: The Masons and the Building of Washington, D.C.*, by David Ovason. Not only does Ovason trace the influence of Freemasonry on the layout of the capital, but he also argues for the influence of the constellation Virgo upon the design – perhaps a handy link with Brown's use in *The Da Vinci Code* of a secret society which worships the female aspect of divinity. The sacred feminine goes international!

Lastly, I should mention one more book that could play a part in our investigation. The legendary esoteric author Manly P. Hall is best-known for his encyclopedic work on occult traditions, *The Secret Teachings of All Ages*. Another of his books, *The Secret Destiny of America,* deserves particular note in regards to *The Solomon Key*. In this intriguing tome, Hall argues that the seeds of a plan for the founding of America "were planted one thousand years before the beginning of the Christian era." Drawing on obscure historical references, *The Secret Destiny of America* investigates the role played by another secret society, the "Rosicrucians", in the founding of America.

Manly Hall believed that the important historical figure of Sir Francis Bacon may be the key to a 'hidden history' regarding the founding of the United States. *The Secret Destiny of America* describes Bacon's own secret society as playing a large part in the establishment of America as a Masonic Republic, free of the constraints of European Christianity and the authoritative monarchies which ruled both France and England at the time. Certainly worthy of further investigation as well.

Puzzles:

Dan Brown's personal interest in cryptography has served him well, with a large part of the success of his books no doubt due to the constant puzzles and codes offered up to the curious reader. The character of Robert Langdon offers an easy method of inserting symbolic references into the plot. The introduction of the cryptographer Sophie Neveu to the mix in *The Da Vinci Code* added yet another option in this department. Incidentally, it will be interesting to see whether Sophie sticks around for the next novel, or disappears in the same way that Vittoria Vetra did after *Angels and Demons* (or perhaps both will make an appearance…a love triangle is always a handy plot device).

Accordingly, *The Solomon Key* is likely to be much of the same in terms of puzzles and challenges for the reader. We should therefore take note of the organizations and history which will be present in this novel, and examine possible codes and ciphers related to them which Dan Brown might be likely to use. For example, which symbols and codes were used by Freemasonry and the Knights Templar? Were any of the historical figures involved known to have an interest in codes? Looking at more recent times, we should obviously include James Sanborn and the Kryptos sculpture in our analysis, as they are directly mentioned in the Internet challenge. Not to mention the fact that the sculpture lies at C.I.A. headquarters in Langley, not far from Washington, D.C.

The other point to note about Dan Brown's cryptographic puzzles is that he regularly includes well-known landmarks and pieces of art within the 'game'. In *The Da Vinci Code* Brown involved historical locations such as the Louvre, Saint Sulpice, and Rosslyn Chapel, as well as famous paintings and sculptures. Considering that he has already mentioned the hidden history of Washington, D.C. as being involved in *The Solomon Key,* we should perhaps seek out some of the more curious landmarks in that area and mark them down as likely locations for scenes in the new novel. We'll discuss this topic further in a later chapter.

The Sacred Feminine:

While the idea of the sacred feminine has only been the focus of one Dan Brown novel, the power of the idea may carry it on into the next book. Many people attribute much of the success of the book to its message of empowerment, in terms of raising the visibility of the female aspect in religious history. This is an especially powerful topic in the modern era, considering that we live in a society dominated by patriarchal religions. Expect Brown to continue with this theme, even if not as the main focus of the new novel. There are interesting details to discuss regarding both Freemasonry and Washington, D.C. in relation to the sacred feminine.

Dichotomies:

As we've already discussed, another Dan Brown signature appears to be the battle between two opposing sides. In *Angels and Demons* it was the science-based Illuminati up against the religion-based Catholic Church. *The Da Vinci Code* stuck to a similar storyline, this time pitting the church – in the form of Opus Dei – against the supporters of the sacred feminine, the secret society known as the Priory of Sion. We already know one of the pair in *The Solomon Key,* Freemasonry. What organization then are we likely to see pitted against the Masons? Perhaps a sect such as the Society of Jesus, better known as the Jesuits, who have had a 'running battle' with Freemasonry and similar organizations for a number of centuries?

Or maybe, with Langley hinted at in the Internet challenge, we will see an intelligence agency involved in this novel? Perhaps we should expect this, as Dan Brown mentioned in an interview subsequent to the publication of *Angels and Demons* that he had "recently learned of another U.S. intelligence agency, more covert even than the National Security Agency"[9], and that it would figure prominently in his next novel. While such an agency didn't eventually show up in *The Da Vinci Code,* it would be more than possible that Brown has saved this group for the first Robert Langdon novel to be set on American soil: *The Solomon Key.*

An Outline Emerges

Like a ship emerging from the fog, we are now beginning to recognize the rough outline of *The Solomon Key.* We know some of the key subjects: Freemasonry, the hidden history of Washington, D.C., the Great Seal and a possible Illuminati conspiracy. We also can predict where some of the details for this outline will come from, with authors previously referenced by Brown writing on some of these very topics. And we know his style. We can now begin to assemble the likely details of one of the most anticipated novels of the decade. Let's start by familiarizing ourselves with the background to the story.

CHAPTER 2

THE ROSICRUCIAN INFLUENCE

In the two existing Robert Langdon novels, Dan Brown has used secret societies as a major theme of each book. In *Angels and Demons* it was the Illuminati, while in *The Da Vinci Code* it was the Priory of Sion. Now we can assume that *The Solomon Key* will deal with Freemasonry. While there are considerable doubts about the pedigree of the Priory of Sion, both the Illuminati and Freemasonry were very real historical groups. Freemasonry has definitely survived into modern times, while the 'Bavarian Illuminati' appears to have survived for less than a decade in the 18th Century – although numerous conspiracy theorists would say they just went 'underground' after this point and not only survive to this day, but are also a major influence behind world events.

Both the Illuminati and Masons are part of a tradition which is often referred to as 'Rosicrucian'. The Rosicrucian groups encompassed numerous beliefs and political allegiances, but can perhaps be best tied together by the similarity of their aspirations.

To understand the beginnings of these groups, we need to travel back in time some five hundred years, and explore the political and religious climate of Europe at the time, as well as the emergence of modern science from the 'Enlightenment' period. This quick diversion through history will prove enormously helpful when it comes to understanding the possible motivations of the Founding Fathers of the United States.

A Divided Europe

The start of the 16th century saw the beginnings of massive turmoil in Europe. The Catholic Church had become morally and financially corrupt. Monarchies throughout Europe had begun asserting their rule in Draconian style, removing constitutional restrictions on their authority. Additionally, as a result of the stress of the rapid changes occurring in societies across the continent, trouble began to ferment just beneath the surface of daily life. Amazingly, it could be argued that a lightning bolt quite literally ignited the impending inferno...

In 1505 a young German man was returning from school when lightning struck the ground near him. Terrified, he immediately made a promise in return for salvation: "Help, St. Anne! I'll become a monk." Soon realizing that he had survived, the 21-year-old Martin Luther kept his word, and dropped out of law school and entered a monastery. However, despite a fervent love for Christianity, it did not take the young man long to become disillusioned with the Church.

Luther's dislike of the endemic greed and corruption within the Catholic Church boiled over in 1517, when he delivered a sermon attacking the practice of selling indulgences. As part of his attack, he also nailed a document to the door of the castle church for debate. Luther's document condemned the Church's greed and secularism. The young Catholic obviously touched a nerve in European society – within two weeks Luther's manifesto had spread throughout Germany, and soon after it was being read and discussed across Europe. The Reformation had begun, and Europe was about to be split into two religious camps – Catholic and Protestant.

In England the Reformation heralded a new era, with Henry VIII finding it politically expedient to break with Rome. Large amounts of Catholic property were taken over by the monarchy, and much of it passed into the hands of the nobility. With such rewards for those supporting the Reformation, the result was obvious. It is in this 'new' England that we find some of the key characters emerging in the beginnings of Rosicrucianism.

THE LAST MAGICIAN

The legendary Elizabethan philosopher John Dee (1527–1609) was the true definition of a 'Renaissance Man'. A respected mathematician, astronomer and geographer, he was also astrologer to Queen Elizabeth and a serious student of alchemy, Kabbalah, and magick. His knowledge of navigation meant that he taught many of the great explorers of the time, and he had the ear of the Queen of England, who held him in high regard.

Despite being a pious Christian, Dee was also fascinated by the occult leanings of the Renaissance period. To many, he is remembered mostly for his attempted communication with angels, a practice still undertaken by modern occultists under the title 'Enochian Magic'. While his activities might seem to us today as heretical, and contradictory to his Christian belief, the religious landscape was of a different kind at that time. The respected scholar Frances Yates points out that during the Renaissance, Hermetic and Kabbalistic studies were not discouraged by the Catholic Church, and in fact cardinals were known to dabble in some of these areas. The status of magick however was far more tentative, with charges of simony always possible.

Dee though would have felt that his magick was of a Christian leaning, as he was attempting to contact the angels, not summoning demons. Indeed, his ultimate goal was to help unify Europe by uncovering the pure religion of the ancients, thus healing any denominational schisms. Yates finds in Dee the beginnings of what she termed the 'Rosicrucian Enlightenment'.[10] With Protestantism allowing more latitude in the tolerance of occult practices, the beginnings of science were nurtured as these 'magicians' experimented in alchemy and natural philosophy. However, Yates says that the occult-leaning Dee was expunged from history as the inspiration for both modern science and Rosicrucianism by those fearing the repercussions of the later witch-hunts.

In *The Rosicrucian Enlightenment*, Frances Yates describes Dee as a "towering figure" who was the major influence behind the original Rosicrucian movement. And the key to this movement was the philosophy of *inclusion*, the idea that humanity could only move forward by being tolerant of all religious attitudes.

THE ADVANCEMENT OF LEARNING

The dawn of the 17th Century was an amazing period of discovery. The heretical idea of Copernicus, that the Earth actually revolved around the Sun, began getting serious attention. The figures of Galileo and Kepler impose their monumental influence upon history. And an English gentleman by the name of Francis Bacon unofficially inaugurated one of the world's greatest scientific institutions.

Sir Francis Bacon (1561-1626) was the youngest of five sons born to Sir Nicholas Bacon, the 'Keeper of the Great Seal' to Queen Elizabeth I. As a man of extraordinary intelligence, Bacon had become dissatisfied with the methods and results of the 'sciences' of the time. Thus he took it upon himself to institute a new mode of learning, in parallel with his influential political and legal career during the reigns of both Elizabeth I and James I. In his 1605 publication *The Advancement of Learning*, Bacon pronounced much of the present state of knowledge to be deficient. He argued for a brotherhood of learning, whereby learned men could exchange ideas independent of their beliefs and political allegiances. Here we find a curious echo of Dee's desire for inclusion, a pan-sophism where knowledge belongs to all men.

Sir Francis Bacon

In his *Novus Organum* ('New Organ'), Bacon put forth his own ideas on how the quest for knowledge could be refined. Intended as a replacement for Aristotle's *Organum*, this book established a far more rigorous scientific procedure, which has become known as the Baconian method. This method of investigation takes note of many possible experimental fallacies, such as the human tendency to see patterns in random systems, incorrect method, and personal bias.

Bacon continued to publish his thoughts on the advancement of knowledge until his bizarre death in 1626. Inspired by the possibility of using snow to preserve meat, Bacon had purchased a chicken from the market and set out to evaluate the hypothesis himself, in true scientific style. However, the process of stuffing the chicken with snow was too much for his fragile health, and he contracted a fatal case of pneumonia from the cold and died soon after. Subsequent to his death, one more extremely influential essay was published, *The New Atlantis*, which we will discuss soon.

THE ROSICRUCIANS ARRIVE

During Bacon's lifetime a number of strange texts suddenly appeared, which despite their obscurity soon began to have a dramatic influence throughout Europe. In 1614 and 1615, in the German town of Kassel, two mysterious manuscripts were published with no hint as to who authored them. Their curious titles were the *Frama Fraternitatis* ("*The Fame of the Praiseworthy Order of the Rosy Cross*") and the *Confessio Fraternitatis* ("*Confession of the Fraternity*").

These manuscripts told the mythical story of a German man named Christian Rosenkreutz, who was born in 1378 and traveled to the Holy Land and the Middle East at age 16. While there, he came across a Utopian-like community, which was governed only by "wise and understanding men". Rosenkreutz was also initiated into occult mysteries and the ancient 'secret wisdom' while on his pilgrimage.

The texts also say that once back in Germany, Rosenkreutz formed the Fraternity of the Rosy Cross in 1407 with a number of like-minded individuals. The group made it their mission to travel the world, spreading the ancient teachings and healing the sick.

Rosenkreutz was said to have died in 1484, at the ripe old age of 106. A small group of initiates continued on with their founder's important work, until in 1604 one of the brethren uncovered a hidden door leading to the tomb of their master. Upon opening a door inscribed with the prophecy "after 120 years I shall open", they found a seven-sided vault filled with symbols, books and other wondrous objects. One of the treasures was the so-called 'Book M', reputed to have been written by King Solomon himself, and in which he recorded "all things past, present, and to come". Standing in the middle of the crypt was a coffin containing the perfectly preserved body of Christian Rosenkreutz. This was taken as a sign that the general public should be made aware of the existence of the Order, and that invitations should be issued for like-minded people to join them in their quest.[11]

The revelation that this secret society was coming forth caused immense excitement across Europe. The changes happening throughout society at that time meant that a lot of people could identify with the Rosicrucian message, of a reconstituted ancient wisdom guiding the people towards a new Utopia. Famous scientists and philosophers attempted to track down or contact the Rosicrucian fraternity, although with no luck. The feeling was that Europe was entering a new age of enlightenment, guided by the 'truth' of the ancients, leading them back to the "Paradisal state before the Fall."[12]

Who were these anonymous brethren committed to reshaping the world? Detailed research has failed to uncover any real members of the original Rosicrucian society, and all evidence points to the documents (as well as the subsequent release *The Chymical Wedding of Christian Rosenkreutz*) being the fictitious creation of a German theologian named Johann Valentin Andreae. No fraternity ever existed – Andreae actually made extensive efforts during his lifetime to correct the misunderstanding that these were literal documents.

Nevertheless, the myth had engendered a reality. Though fiction, they provided a model for what was needed in the material world. A major part of the Utopia prophesized by the Rosicrucians was the recommendation that learned men of different backgrounds collaborate for the good of all mankind. Strangely enough, this is exactly what happened soon after in England.

THE INVISIBLE COLLEGE

At the time of his death, Sir Francis Bacon had been working on a Utopian myth of his own, *The New Atlantis*. Though incomplete, it was nevertheless published in 1627, one year after his passing and just over a decade after the release of the Rosicrucian documents in Germany. In *The New Atlantis*, Bacon set out his dream of a perfect society where religion and science co-exist in harmony. It tells the story of navigators who discover a new land, in which they find this perfect society. Within this culture, there is a group of priest-scientists organized in a college called Solomon's House, which is dedicated to the quest for illuminating knowledge and the advancement of humanity. The necessary link back to ancient wisdom is made here, with Bacon also saying that the New Atlantis has possession of some of the lost works of King Solomon.

The curious thing about *The New Atlantis* is that, despite there being no references to the Fraternity of the Rosy Cross in its pages, it is quite obvious that it is a Rosicrucian document. Frances Yates has raised solid evidence to prove this point, not least that one of the officials of the Utopian Atlantis wears a white turban "with a small red cross on the top."[13] Indeed, Solomon's House sounds extremely similar to the Rosicrucian fraternity.

Yates points out that another author by the name of John Heydon recorded his recognition of this similarity three decades later in his *Holy Guide*. This book was basically an adaptation of *The New Atlantis*, except in Heydon's version the 'House of Solomon' is replaced by "the wise Men of the Society of the Rosicrucians."[14] And he expands Bacon's 'lost works of Solomon' to include the legendary 'Book M' found in the tomb of Christian Rosenkreutz.

The obvious question to be raised is: was *The New Atlantis* inspired by the Rosicrucian manifestos, or were the manifestos originally written in response to Bacon's earlier work and as such appeared to presage Bacon's Utopian allegory? A third possibility also emerges, one that we will explore further in the next chapter: that both Bacon and Andreae were influenced by an earlier tradition.

The publication of Sir Francis Bacon's *The New Atlantis*, in combination with the Rosicrucian Manifestos, led to an almost feverish expectancy that a great change was afoot. Utopians gathered in England, the home of Bacon. The Utopian Samuel Hartlib wrote his own fiction, *A Description of the Famous Kingdom of Macaria*, and addressed it to the English Parliament, confidently predicting that they would "lay the corner stone of the worlds happinesse." The great educator, Comenius, professed his wish that agents of change begin spreading throughout the known world, and intriguingly added that these people must be guided by an order...

> *...so that each of them may know what he has to do, and*
> *for whom and when and with what assistance, and may*

set about his business in a manner which will make for the public benefit.[15]

However, the Utopian dream was to be put on hold when England descended into civil war in 1642, leading to the abolition of the monarchy and the beginnings of the protectorate of Oliver Cromwell. Or at least the public face of the Utopians disappeared, as around this time we see the first records emerging of an 'Invisible College'. The Scottish chemist Robert Boyle, who went on to develop the eponymous Boyle's Law (that the volume of a gas varies inversely with the pressure), mentions this society in a letter dated February 1647:

> *The best on't is, that the cornerstones of the Invisible or (as they term themselves) the Philosophical College, do now and then honour me with their company…men of so capacious and searching spirits…persons that endeavour to put narrow-mindedness out of countenance, by the practice of so extensive a charity that it reaches unto everything called man, and nothing less than an universal good-will can content it…they take the whole body of mankind to their care.*

The Invisible College is believed to be the antecedent to the more famous scientific institution, the Royal Society, which has boasted some of the greatest minds of the past few centuries (Isaac Newton being one of many). Inaugurated in 1660, at the time of the restoration of the throne to England, the Society included a number of both parliamentarians and monarchists, brought together in the quest for knowledge. Frances Yates points out that at this point, the goals of the organization appear to have changed, at least outwardly:

*..the situation was tricky. There were many subjects which
had to be avoided: utopian schemes for reform belonged to
the revolutionary past which it was now better to forget...
witch-scares were not altogether a thing of the past.*[16]

The Royal Society is now viewed by many as the inspiration
for modern science. To be sure, a number of members were
rationalists, following in the mode of Francis Bacon. But
also present were alchemists, hermeticists and Kabbalists
– Newton himself was an alchemist who did not believe in
the Catholic doctrine of the Holy Trinity. And lurking beneath
the surface of the Royal Society was another secret society,
one which returns us to the central topic of Dan Brown's
The Solomon Key: Freemasonry.

CHAPTER 3

THE MASONIC
BROTHERHOOD

Now that we have a basic understanding of the background to the Rosicrucian movement, we should be better able to understand the origins of Freemasonry. Freemasonry is often described as "a peculiar system of morality veiled in allegory and illustrated by symbols." It is a secret society, complete with coded words and secret handshakes, which uses a graded system of initiation – thus maintaining a hierarchical system of members who are exposed to 'deeper mysteries' as they move further up the ladder. The 'system of morality' uses as its metaphor the theme of the stone mason, using raw materials and certain tools to construct a polished temple, in conjunction with legends originating in the Judaic tradition.

These legends tell of the building of Solomon's Temple, an event mentioned in Judaic commentaries, the Christian Old Testament, as well as in Islamic sources. After succeeding his father David, Solomon decided to build a great temple, and enlisted the help of the king of the neighboring country of Tyre:

> *Thou knowest how that David my father could not build an*
> *house unto the name of the Lord his God for the wars which*
> *were about him on every side, until the Lord put them under*
> *the soles of his feet. But now the Lord my God hath given me*
> *rest on every side, so that there is neither adversary nor evil*
> *occurrent. And, behold, I purpose to build an house unto*
> *the name of the Lord my God...*[17]

In the Old Testament commentary, we find present two elements which would become important parts of Masonic iconography – the twin pillars named Jachin and Boaz, and the designation of an architect/builder named Hiram as 'the widow's son':

> *King Solomon sent for Hiram of Tyre; he was the son of*
> *a widow of the tribe of Naphtali but his father had been*
> *a Tyrian, a bronzeworker. He came to King Solomon*
> *and did all this work for him: He cast two bronze*
> *pillars...and he set up the right pillar, and called the*
> *name thereof Jachin: and he set up the left pillar, and*
> *called the name thereof Boaz.*[18]

The legends of Masonry tell more about this Hiram than is mentioned in the Bible commentary. Naming him as 'Hiram Abiff', the Craft mythology sees him as a master architect, skilled in geometry and mathematics. Hiram, as the Master Mason, presided over three grades of workers on the Temple – apprentices, fellows and masters – with particular handshakes and secret words being used to designate each level of Mason.

Masonic legend tells that near the completion of Solomon's Temple, Hiram was praying alone when he was confronted by three 'fellows' seeking the 'Master's word'. When Hiram refused to pass on this secret information, he was then assaulted by the trio. The legend tells that each of the villains inflicted a particular wound upon Hiram at three of the cardinal points of the Temple (north, south and west): he is hit on the head by a hammer, as well as on each temple by a plumb and a level. Hiram staggers to the exit on the eastern side of the Temple, but collapses and dies.

The murderers proceed to hide the body of Hiram, burying it beneath a sprig of acacia. It is not until seven days later that the corpse is found, at which point it is exhumed and reinterred with proper ceremony. At the funeral, the Master Masons all wear white gloves and aprons, a symbolic gesture to show that they are not stained with the murdered man's blood.

While it is difficult for us to attach a deeper meaning to this legend, there is little doubt that it is a 'blind' which disguises some secret. Perhaps it is an allegory referring to nature religions, or maybe it is a coded reference to the archaic ritual killings used to consecrate a new building in the ancient world. Whatever its meaning, the legend and many of the symbols that go with it (the acacia, the apron, the cardinal directions in the Temple) are of profound importance to the core of Freemasonry.

As an aside, it is interesting to note that Michael Baigent and Richard Leigh, in their book *The Temple and the Lodge*, raise the possibility that the Temple of Solomon was built in honor of the Phoenician mother goddess Astarte – the 'Queen of Heaven'.[19] They cite evidence from the Old Testament, which explicitly says that Solomon became a follower of Astarte. It is also said that the well-known 'Song of Solomon' is in fact a hymn to Astarte. In terms of Dan Brown's use of the 'sacred feminine' theme, this may be something given special attention in *The Solomon Key*.

Modern Freemasonry has become somewhat of an enigma. Described by some as the secret power behind world governments, it is conversely thought of by others to simply be an out-of-date 'old boys club' performing rituals of which members have no understanding. It claims a pedigree going back to ancient Egypt and the Temple of Solomon, and yet historical evidence suggests it is a (relatively) modern invention. It espouses an egalitarian doctrine free from prejudice, and yet it maintains its secrecy, uses an internal hierarchy, and is restricted to male applicants. These contradictory attributes of Freemasonry, though perhaps overstated, are often the main sources of criticism of the 'Craft'.

How could Freemasonry fit into Dan Brown's story about the hidden history of America? There is a simple answer, which is that a number of the Founding Fathers of the United States were either Freemasons, or were closely influenced by the organization. And if I am correct in my predictions for *The Solomon Key*, Dan Brown will expand upon the idea that the Founding Fathers were profoundly influenced by the Rosicrucian ideal of a Utopia where humanity joins together in the search for illumination. Let's see if we can connect the dots.

THE OFFICIAL HISTORY

The official history of Freemasonry begins with the inauguration of the Grand Lodge in London in 1717. The Grand Lodge acted as a governing body for the many individual lodges, establishing standard practices to which other lodges were directed to conform. Initially, there were two levels of initiation: the 'Entered Apprentice', which was followed by 'Fellow Craft'. Soon after a third 'degree' was added, that of the 'Master Mason' (the intense questioning of the candidate which occurs during the initiation ceremony now gives its name to any intense interrogation: to be 'given the third degree'). These three standard degrees are commonly referred to as 'blue' Masonry, and are based on the legend of Hiram as mentioned earlier.

The official movement soon spread into Europe, with the French educated classes showing a particular affinity for the fraternal society. The first Grand Lodge of France was founded in Paris at some point during the 1730s. Once in France, the Craft began to evolve somewhat, with the addition of chivalric themes and mystical elements to the Mason mythos. Out of this development came a new species of Freemasonry – the 'Scottish Rite' – which claimed a heritage back to the Knights Templar.

You may be curious as to why a French system of Masonry became known as Scottish Rite. This is due largely to the influence of a Scottish émigré named Andrew Michael Ramsay, who claimed in an introductory speech to initiates – referred to as the 'Oration' – that Masonry arose out of the Crusades and the Templar organization, and that this authentic tradition was preserved by Scottish Masonry. New rites and degrees were added to the basic Craft initiation, based on a mystical story relating back to the building of Solomon's Temple. In Scottish Rite, there are now 33 degrees (32 of which are by initiation, the last degree is an honorary degree bestowed upon the 'worthy'). These added degrees are referred to as 'red' Masonry.

Other species of Masonry continued to be spawned as the Craft spread across Europe, into Germany, Prussia and elsewhere. German Masonry was dominated for a time by the 'Strict Observance', founded in 1760, and which once again emphasized a Templar tradition behind the brotherhood. Later modifications included the 'York Rite' and 'Rectified Scottish Rite', and some lodges started to incorporate Egyptian influences as well.

A secret society that failed to observe strict Christian doctrine was bound to arouse the suspicion of the Church, based on the possibility of a conspiracy to undermine their authority. Sure enough, Pope Clement XII condemned Freemasonry in 1738, as did Pope Benedict XIV in 1751. While these papal orders were not implemented by local authorities, suspicions about the Craft continued, with Lodges barely being tolerated in many regions. However, despite continued negative publicity throughout its history, today there are more than 10,000 Masonic lodges covering practically every corner of the globe.

Masonry's Hidden History

So much for the accepted view of Masonic history. Let's now turn to some of Dan Brown's probable sources for the 'alternative history' of the brotherhood, which are likely to make an appearance in *The Solomon Key*. The primary references we'll use on this subject, for the reasons discussed in an earlier chapter, are:

- *Holy Blood, Holy Grail*, by Michael Baigent, Richard Leigh, and Henry Lincoln
- *The Temple and the Lodge*, by Michael Baigent and Richard Leigh
- *The Templar Revelation*, by Lynn Picknett and Clive Prince
- *The Hiram Key*, by Robert Lomas and Chris Knight

Each of these books deals explicitly with the theory that Freemasonry arose from the Templar tradition.

When Andrew Ramsay enunciated the connection between the Craft and the Knights Templar, it was certainly not fashionable to do so. This group of crusading knights – under the official name of the 'Poor Knights of Christ and the Temple of Solomon' – had been disbanded in the early 14th century under accusations of debauchery and sacrilege.

On Friday the 13th 1307, King Philippe IV of France had ordered the arrest of all Templars in his domains. The operation was done under an amazing veil of secrecy, with sealed orders being opened by the King's men only shortly before the action to minimize the Templars' foreknowledge of the impending catastrophe. The Catholic 'Inquisition' then took over where Philippe left off, and Templars throughout Europe were interrogated, imprisoned, and often executed with bizarre accusations being leveled against them. The Pope dissolved the Templar order in 1312, and in 1314 Jacques de Molay, the last Grand-Master of the Knights Templar, was burned at the stake.[20]

Under intense interrogations Templar knights admitted to strange behaviour, and rumors began to circulate about the true nature of this supposedly 'holy' Order. Charges against them included spitting and trampling on the cross, of obscene kisses during initiations, and that they worshipped a devil called 'Baphomet'. After so many centuries, it is difficult now to really know which charges may have had some substance. As Baigent, Leigh and Lincoln point out in *Holy Blood, Holy Grail*, trying to do so by studying the records of the Inquisition is a little like trying to get the facts about the activities of the French resistance during World War II by studying the records of the Gestapo.[21]

Nevertheless, certain accusations seem to have had some basis. For example, the worship of 'Baphomet' turns up regularly, too many times to be a coincidence. Dan Brown mentions it in *The Da Vinci Code*, describing Baphomet as a "pagan fertility god associated with the creative force of reproduction." According to him, the Templars honored Baphomet by encircling a stone replica of his horned head whilst chanting prayers. Brown also has his characters decrypt the word 'Baphomet' via the Atbash Cipher, which translates it into 'Sophia', the Greek word for 'wisdom'.

Despite the apparent ingenuity of Robert Langdon and company, this decryption was actually first publicized by Dr Hugh Schonfield in *The Essene Odyssey*. In his book, published in 1985, Schonfield discusses the Jewish rebel sect known as the Essenes, who are thought by some to have constructed the Dead Sea settlement and also authored the now-famous ancient scrolls found there. The Essenes employed codes in some of their writings, one of which is the Atbash Cipher. The cipher is a straight substitution between two Hebrew alphabets, one written forward and the other in reverse (first for last, second for second-last etc). Hugh Schonfield applied the Atbash to what he believed was the "artificial name Baphomet", and was surprised to find it revealed the name of the Goddess of Wisdom. The implication of Schonfield's discovery is that the Templars may have been the protectors of Essene secrets, and may also have had a reverence for the mystery religions of the ancient goddesses.

This possibility of a Templar fascination with the 'sacred feminine' may be backed up by Andrew Ramsay's 'Oration', mentioned above, given in 1737 and linking Masonry and the Templars. For in it he says:

> *Yes, sirs, the famous festivals of Ceres at Eleusis, of Isis in Egypt, of Minerva at Athens, of Urania amongst the Phenicians, and of Diana in Scythia were connected with ours. In those places mysteries were celebrated which concealed many vestiges of the ancient religion of Noah and the Patriarchs.*[22]

While the revelation that the Scottish Rite identifies itself with the ancient mystery schools of the sacred goddesses is certainly a pleasant surprise, it is also pertinent to note that Ramsay does not condone any 'Hieros Gamos'-like practices – indeed he gives such corruptions as a reason for the exclusion of females from the Craft:

> *The source of these infamies was the admission to the nocturnal assemblies of persons of both sexes in contravention*

of the primitive usages. It is in order to prevent similar abuses that women are excluded from our Order. We are not so unjust as to regard the fair sex as incapable of keeping a secret. But their presence might insensibly corrupt the purity of our maxims and manners.[23]

Schonfield's discovery of the Atbash cipher also creates a link between two organizations more than a millennium apart. So what Essene secrets might the Templars have been privy to? In *The Hiram Key*, Chris Knight and Robert Lomas argue that ideas found in the Dead Sea Scrolls are very similar to Freemasonry, and this proves a continuity of tradition from Essene to Freemason through the Templars. However, it should be mentioned that in another of Dan Brown's 'sources', *The Templar Revelation,* authors Lynn Picknett and Clive Prince disagree on this point, as they believe the Dead Sea Scrolls are in fact part of the library of the Jerusalem Temple, which was destroyed by Rome in 70 AD.

Interestingly, one of the Dead Sea Scrolls, known as the 'Copper Scroll', makes reference to twenty four separate hoards of treasure reputedly secreted away beneath the Temple.[24] This cache is said to be comprised of treasure of all types – bullion, sacred objects, and a number of scrolls as well. And the Knights Templar, while crusading in the Holy Land, were known to have stationed themselves in the vicinity of the Temple Mount. Were they there to search for the treasure?

It would seem so. In the book *Digging Up Jerusalem,* authored by respected archaeologist Kathleen Kenyon, we are told that a group of the British Army Royal Engineers surveyed and excavated the Temple Mount in the late 19th Century.[25] And, according to the testimony of Robert Brydon, the Templar archivist for Scotland, this British Army contingent unearthed already existing tunnels in which were found a part of a Templar sword, the remains of a lance, and a Templar cross. No treasure was found. Did the Templars find it first?

Dan Brown, in *The Da Vinci Code*, assumes they found something and writes his novel accordingly. In his words, "four chests of documents" were found under the site of Solomon's Temple, "documents that have been the object of countless Grail quests throughout history" – perhaps including a text written by Jesus himself and the 'diary' of Mary Magdalene recording her personal relationship with Jesus. These are Brown's 'Sangreal' documents, which form part of the Holy Grail along with the body of Mary Magdalene.

Knight and Lomas offer the perfect link between *The Da Vinci Code* and *The Solomon Key*, if Dan Brown wishes to take advantage of it. In *The Second Messiah*, they provide an alternative history to the naming of America, which involves the Essenes, Knights Templar and Freemasons:

> *Josephus records that the Essenes (and therefore the Jerusalem Church) believed that good souls reside beyond the ocean to the west, in a region that is not oppressed with storms of rain, snow or intense heat, but has refreshing gentle breezes.*

> *This was also the description given by a people called the Mandaeans who have lived in Southern Iraq since they left Jerusalem shortly after the crucifixion of Jesus, in order to escape the purges of Paul. These Jews left Jerusalem in the first century AD and, according to their traditional history, John the Baptist was the first leader of the Nasoreans and Jesus was a subsequent leader who betrayed special secrets that had been entrusted to him. The Mandaeans still conduct baptism in the river, have special handshakes and practise rituals said to resemble those of Freemasonry. For*

them this wonderful land across the sea has only the purest spirits, so perfect that mortal eyes cannot see them. This wonderful place is marked by a star called Merica, that sits in the sky above it.

We believe that this star and the mythical land below it were known to the Knights Templar from the scrolls that they discovered, and that they sailed in search of 'La Merica' or, as we now know it, America, immediately after their Order had been outlawed.

In *Holy Blood, Holy Grail* the Essenes are described as a mystically oriented Jewish sect, with both Greek and Egyptian influences. Like the Rosicrucian tradition, they were interested in healing, and esoteric studies such as astrology and the Kabbalah. In light of Dan Brown's hint that *The Solomon Key* would involve an "ultrasecret numerology sect", we should sit up and take notice that the members of the reclusive Essene community were also said to have been keen followers of the teachings of Pythagoras, with a substantial devotion to numerology.[26]

Beyond the Atbash Cipher, there also seems to be evidence that the Templars dabbled in alchemy, mysticism and the Kabbalah, much like the Essenes. Interestingly, especially in terms of our investigation, they may also have held as an ideal the possibility of uniting all religions and nations. In light of these attributes, it would seem that the Templars were very much in the Rosicrucian tradition. The fact that the Templars wore as their insignia a red cross might be evidence that the author of the Rosicrucian tracts was attempting to directly link the fraternity to the Knights of Solomon's Temple. Especially so when we consider that Sir Francis Bacon portrayed his priests of the 'House of Solomon' wearing a red cross on their turban. However, how do we explain the three centuries between the suppression of the Knights Templar and the appearance of the Rosicrucian manifestos?

THE TEMPLARS LIVE

Despite the great secrecy surrounding Philippe's action against the Order, it would seem that the Templars – to some extent at least – knew what was coming. Jacques de Molay allegedly called in many of the Order's documents shortly before the arrests and had them burnt. A young knight who withdrew from the Order at this time was told he was extremely wise to do so, as a catastrophe was coming.[27]

In *Holy Blood, Holy Grail* the authors claim that a certain group of knights – all connected to the organization's treasurer – disappeared before the 'October surprise', taking with them the remaining documents and treasure of the Temple. According to one rumor, they boarded a fleet of eighteen ships at La Rochelle and were never heard of again.

Michael Baigent and Richard Leigh pick up the trail of these missing knights in their book about Freemasonry, *The Temple and the Lodge*. They assert that these knights may well have fled to Scotland, taking sides with Robert the Bruce in his fight against England. They were not the first to arrive at such a conclusion, with Templar historians of the 19th Century coming to much the same conclusion:

> *The Templars...perhaps found a refuge in the little army of the excommunicated King Robert, whose fear of offending the French monarch would doubtless be vanquished by his desire to secure a few capable men-at-arms as recruits*[28]

The Masonic rite of the Strict Observance, created by Baron Karl von Hund in the late 18th Century, also claims that the Templars escaped to Scotland.

Baigent and Leigh develop a thread which has the Templar tradition morphing into the beginnings of Freemasonry. As part of their argument, they cite the architectural wonder that is Rosslyn Chapel, built in the period 1440–1480. A prominent setting in Dan Brown's *The Da Vinci Code*, this small chapel is filled with esoteric and pagan symbols carved into every spare section of wall and ceiling. Curiously, there are also some motifs that point to Freemasonry. For example, one of three heads carved in the ceiling, with head wound clearly visible, is referred to as the 'Widow's Son', a standard Masonic appellation first given to the Master Mason Hiram. The two beautifully carved pillars within the chapel are another echo of Masonic symbolism, that of the twin pillars of Jachin and Boaz. Also, according to *The Second Messiah* – the sequel to Lomas and Knight's *The Hiram Key* – Rosslyn was actually built to be a replica of the Jerusalem Temple.

In *The Second Messiah*, Knight and Lomas also stumbled over another astonishing discovery. After a detailed inspection of the carvings at Rosslyn, they came across one that illustrated perfectly a certain stage of the initiation rite for a candidate in Freemasonry.[29] This was a startling revelation, as it was evidence of a Masonic rite some two centuries before the first recorded initiation. Even more surprising was the fact that the person doing the initiation had a cross on the front of his robe – a Templar. Linking Masonry with the Templars and Essenes, Knight and Lomas believe that Rosslyn Chapel was in fact built to house the Essene scrolls, which they think were found by the Templars in Jerusalem:

> *The obvious was starting to descend upon us and we both had a simultaneous attack of goose pimples. Rosslyn was not*

a simple chapel; it was a post-Templar shrine built to house
the scrolls found by Hugues de Payen and his team under
the Holy of Holies of the last Temple at Jerusalem! Beneath
our feet was the most priceless treasure in Christendom.[30]

They state their opinion that William St Clair, builder of Rosslyn Chapel, secreted the treasure and then left coded instructions in the Holy Royal Arch degree of Masonry. Referring to the possible outline of a Seal of Solomon in the floor-plan of the chapel (which Dan Brown employed in *The Da Vinci Code)*, they point at this Masonic definition of the instantly recognizable hexagram shape:

The Companion's Jewel of the Royal Arch is a double
triangle, sometimes called the Seal of Solomon, within a
circle of gold; at the bottom is a scroll bearing the words,
'Nil nisi clavis deest' – "Nothing but the key is wanting[31]

Whether Knight and Lomas are correct is still not known. However, Dan Brown certainly used the idea to his advantage in *The Da Vinci Code*, indicating that the 'Holy Grail' was hidden by the Seal of Solomon on the floor of Rosslyn Chapel. And considering the above quote, we might begin to understand the territory *The Solomon Key* will explore.

Dan Brown even cites the Royal Arch Degree in *The Da Vinci Code*, in a passage where Langdon describes the use of *la clef de voûte* (the key to the vault). He draws directly on the research of Knight and Lomas by describing this key as the central, wedge-shaped stone at the top of an arch which locks the pieces together and carries all the weight. And perhaps gives access to a secret chamber...

Baigent and Leigh argue that Rosslyn Chapel is evidence that the Templar tradition became ensconced in the 'safe haven' of Scotland after the suppression by Philippe IV of France, through a transfer to the secret initiations of Masonry. It is interesting to note other evidence that the Craft already existed around this time. For example, *The Templar Revelation* cites the evidence of an alchemical treatise dating to the 1450s – the same timeframe as the construction of Rosslyn Chapel – which explicitly uses the term 'Freemason'.[32] Baigent and Leigh also refer to a manuscript from 1410 regarding a stonemason's guild, which mentions the "king's son of Tyre" and connects him with an ancient science from before the Great Flood, which was preserved in the teachings of Pythagoras and Hermes.[33]

According to *The Temple and the Lodge,* the Craft entered England proper in 1603 when the Scottish King James VI was crowned King of England, and Scottish aristocrats – the keepers of Masonry – moved south with their master. Again, it is pertinent to note the chronology, this being the exact time that both Francis Bacon and the Rosicrucian manifestos began coming to the fore.

ROSICRUCIANS TO FREEMASONS

What links can be found between the Rosicrucian philosophy and Freemasonry? Firstly, like the Utopian dream of the Rosicrucians, the Craft promotes the doctrine that all men are brothers, who should be united in religious devotion to a higher being simply referred to as the 'Great Architect of the Universe'. In one of Freemasonry's guiding works, the *Book of Constitutions,* this is pronounced in the following manner:

> *A Mason is oblig'd, by his Tenure, to obey the Moral Law;*
> *and if he rightly understands the Art, he will never be a*
> *stupid Atheist, nor an irreligious Libertine... 'tis now thought*

more expedient only to oblige…to that Religion in which all Men agree, leaving their particular Opinions to themselves; that is, to be good Men and true, or Men of Honour and Honesty, by whatever Denominations or Persuasions they may be distinguish'd.[34]

The rules of the Mason's lodge include restricted discussion of both religion and politics, in order to help attain this goal – and perhaps as a method of easing the minds of the religious and secular authorities. Despite this professed avoidance of politics, however, Freemasonry has regularly played a part in democratic revolutions and interventions over the centuries – for example, in France, Mexico and Italy, and as we shall see in the United States as well. This may well be related back to the Utopian desire first professed by the Rosicrucian tradition.

In the way of more concrete evidence, a poem published at Edinburgh in 1638 directly links the two organizations. Remember, this is only two decades after the appearance of the Rosicrucian tracts and eighty years before the official inauguration of the Grand Lodge in London. Written by Henry Adamson of Perth, the poem reads:

For what we do presage is not in grosse,
For we be brethren of the Rosie Crosse:
We have the Mason word and second sight,
Things for to come we can foretell aright…[35]

In 1824 an essay appeared in *London Magazine* titled "Historico-Critical Inquiry into the Origins of the Rosicrucians and the Freemasons". The author, Thomas de Quincey, makes clear his belief that "no college or lodge of Rosicrucian brethren…can be shown from historical records to have ever been established". However, he does believe that the influence of the Rosicrucian manifestos inspired the creation of secret societies such as Freemasonry:

> *The original Free-Masons were a society that arose out of the Rosicrucian mania, certainly within the thirteen years from 1633 to 1646, and probably between 1633 and 1640.*[36]

Both de Quincey and Adamson mark a time frame that we covered in an earlier chapter – a decade after the publication of Sir Francis Bacon's *The New Atlantis* when the Utopians were petitioning the English parliament. If we look closely we see perhaps a hint that men like Samuel Hartlib were already involved in Masonry. In 1640 he wrote of his desire that the parliament "will lay the *cornerstone* of the worlds happinesse."

The idea of a cornerstone as signifying the beginnings of a new construction are a potent symbol in Freemasonry, and Hartlib's choice of metaphor could well be an indication of a secret affiliation. So we may then also ask about the affiliations of Robert Boyle, as in 1647 he remarks in a letter "that the *cornerstones* of the Invisible…College, do now and then honor me with their company."

If so, he would not be the only member of the 'Invisible College' to be a card-carrying Freemason. In *The Rosicrucian Enlightenment*, Frances Yates points out that two of the earliest recorded initiations into speculative Masonry were also in the 1640s. One was Robert Moray, one of the main influences behind the establishment of the Royal Society in 1660, who was inducted into the mason's lodge of Edinburgh in May 1641. Five years later it is recorded that the alchemist and antiquarian Elias Ashmole, another of the foundation members of the Royal Society, became a Mason at a lodge in Lancashire.[37]

The name of the lodge in Lancashire where Ashmole was received is revealing: the 'House of Solomon.'[38] Here we find direct evidence that the Freemasons of the time were heavily influenced by Sir Francis Bacon's Utopian myth, *The New Atlantis*, remembering that the priests of the 'House of Solomon' on the Utopian island were the equivalent of the Rosicrucians. And Bacon's secret society may have been directly linked with the Templar tradition.

While the 'English experiment' dissolved with the advent of the civil war, the Utopian ideal of a brotherhood united in the quest for illumination continued through the Royal Society, and ultimately Freemasonry. A century later, on the other side of the globe, a group of Freemasons may have begun a second experiment which would change the world...

CHAPTER 4

THE MASONIC FOUNDATIONS OF AMERICA

In 1897, an American army officer named Charles Totten wrote "there are mysteries connected with the birth of this Republic."[39] Totten had been investigating the strange iconography of the Great Seal of the United States, and through his research became convinced that the birth of the American nation could be related to the vision of Francis Bacon's *The New Atlantis*, who provided some financial support for the early Virginia colony. Totten's remark is, surprisingly, somewhat of an understatement.

On the 18th September, 1793, President George Washington took part in a Masonic ceremony to officially mark the beginning of the construction of the Capitol in Washington, D.C. Wearing his own Masonic apron, the first President of the United States of America marched to the site with the members of a number of local Freemasonry lodges, and then descended into the construction pit which housed the cornerstone of the building. Washington placed a silver plate upon the cornerstone, and then made the standard Masonic 'offerings' of corn, wine and oil. The Masonic tools carried by Washington on this momentous day are still held at a lodge in the District of Columbia.[40]

To many of us today, it seems strange that such an important day in the history of the United States of America would have such an overtly Masonic theme. What sort of importance did Freemasonry have in the founding of the United States? That is a question which Dan Brown looks likely to explore in *The Solomon Key* – as we have already pointed out, he is on record as saying the upcoming Robert Langdon novel is on the topic of Freemasonry and "explores the hidden history of our nation's capital."

The idea that the United States may have been founded as a 'Masonic Republic' is not a new one. We have already seen that Charles Totten considered it in 1897. The esoteric author Manly P. Hall also claims in his book, *The Secret Destiny of America*, that Sir Francis Bacon himself decided that the Utopian dream could be realized in North America.[41]

In their book *Talisman*, authors Robert Bauval and Graham Hancock point out research by historian Ron Heisler which suggests another link between Utopian visions in Europe and the new colony in America. Heisler discovered that the German occultist – and staunch Rosicrucian – Michael Maier was in close contact with a number of individuals connected with the Virginia Company. This group of wealthy individuals had been granted a royal charter by James I in 1606, basically giving them unlimited power of government in the colony. This charter had been drafted by none other than…Francis Bacon. Heisler believes that Maier's alchemical tract *Atalanta Fugiens* "may have been deeply inspired by the Utopian vision of America."

American scholar Donald R. Dickson provides another link between the Utopian dreamers and the Virginian settlement in his book *The Tessera of Antilia*. Dickson's investigations uncovered the existence of a Utopian society known as 'Antilia', which counted Rosicrucian instigator Valentin Andreae among its participants. Inspired by both the Rosicrucian tracts as well as Francis Bacon's writings, this brotherhood at one point contemplated emigrating *en masse* to Virginia in order to found their Utopian society.

It is clear then that some Utopian thinkers in Europe saw the Virginia colony as an ideal location for a 'new beginning'. In terms of our investigation it is worthwhile noting that in *The Temple and the Lodge*, Michael Baigent and Richard Leigh – the authors who provided the anagram for Leigh Teabing's name in *The Da Vinci Code* – mention that according to some traditions, a form of Freemasonry arrived in the New World two decades before Bacon even published *The New Atlantis*, and actively worked to promote the Utopian society dreamed of by Rosicrucian thinkers.[42]

In any case, the first documented Freemason to settle in the United States was a Scotsman by the name of John Skene. Initiated at a lodge in Aberdeen sometime before 1671, Skene settled in the New World in 1682, going on to become deputy governor of New Jersey. However, there are no records of a lodge in the United States prior to the formation of the Grand Lodge in London in 1717. What is interesting though, is that the first documented evidence referring to Freemasonry in America was printed in *The Pennsylvania Gazette* in 1730 – by one Benjamin Franklin.

BENJAMIN FRANKLIN

Few people could claim to possess the talents of Dr Benjamin Franklin. A journalist and author, he published and wrote for his own newspaper, *The Pennsylvania Gazette*, during the first half of the 18th Century. With a group of like-minded individuals, he also founded Pennsylvania's first library in 1732 and devoted himself to the spread of knowledge and learning.

Franklin is also widely known for his scientific work and inventions, with his famous experiment of flying a kite during a storm (to demonstrate that lightning was a form of electricity) becoming part of popular folklore. To complement his reputation as one of the great scientists of the 18th Century, he also invented two common devices still used today – the lightning rod and bifocal spectacles.

Franklin was also a diplomat and power-broker who was of profound importance to the founding of the United States. His role in discussions between England and the colonies on various matters began in the 1750s, making the suggestion of a union of the colonies as far back as 1754. In 1765, when the British Parliament passed the infamous Stamp Act (a tax levy on a wide variety of documents in the American colonies, which was a trigger for the separatist movement that led to the American Revolution), Franklin actively opposed it. In 1775 he was elected a member of the Continental Congress, and played a key role in the Declaration of Independence, despite his personal preference to remain affiliated with the British empire.

Franklin was posted as the new nation's diplomat to France in 1776, and conducted his role with great success. He was instrumental in securing a military alliance with France, and negotiated the peace with Great Britain via the Treaty of Paris in 1783. He is the only Founding Father who is a signatory to the three foundation documents of the United States: the Declaration of Independence, the Treaty of Paris and the United States Constitution.

Benjamin Franklin was also a Freemason and a Deist. He was initiated in February 1731, and rose to the rank of Provincial Grand Master of Pennsylvania by 1734. As a publisher, he was in a unique position to aid the cause of Freemasonry in the New World. He published Anderson's *Book of Constitutions,* the authoritative Masonic document, in 1734. In 1756 he had been inducted into the Royal Society in England, which we have seen was heavily Masonic and perhaps Rosicrucian in nature.[43] And in 1778, while in France, he was initiated into the highly influential 'Neuf Soeurs' ('Nine Sisters') lodge in Paris, which would boast Voltaire, Lafayette, Court de Gebelin and numerous instigators of the French Revolution as members.[44] He was also a friend of the Englishman Sir Francis Dashwood – founder of the Hellfire Club.

Manly P. Hall, in *The Secret Destiny of America,* claims that Benjamin Franklin was part of the 'Order of the Quest', the secret movement to construct a Utopian democracy in the New World:

> *Men bound by a secret oath to labor in the cause of world democracy decided that in the American colonies they would plant the roots of a new way of life... Benjamin Franklin exercised an enormous psychological influence in Colonial politics as the appointed spokesman of the unknown philosophers; he did not make laws, but his words became law.*

Franklin had been a Freemason for almost fifty years by the time he signed the Declaration of Independence. What other Masonic influences can we find in the founding of the United States?

George Washington

As we have already noted above, George Washington was most definitely a Freemason. The commander-in-chief of the colonial

George Washington Masonic Memorial (© J. Alison)

armies during the American Revolutionary War was initiated into the lodge at Fredericksburg on the 4th of November 1752. He was 'raised' as a Master Mason only a year later. In 1777 he was offered the position of Grand Master of the planned Grand Lodge of the United States, but he declined (quite ironically) on the basis that he was not qualified for such a high office.[45]

There is little doubt that Washington would have been more than capable of filling this position – his refusal to accept was based more on a genuine modesty which remained in evidence throughout his life. He refused to be paid for his military service, and left the room when John Adams recommended him for the position of commander-in-chief of the Continental Army. Despite accepting the post, Washington told the Continental Congress that he was unworthy of the honor. He was also reluctant to be seen using his power as President of the United States. Thomas Jefferson wrote of him:

> *The moderation and virtue of a single character probably prevented this Revolution from being closed, as most others have been, by a subversion of that liberty it was intended to establish.*

In 1788, the year before becoming the first President of the United States, Washington did become Master of the Alexandria lodge in Washington, D.C., today known as the Alexandria Washington Lodge No. 22. The lodge became the site of the George Washington Masonic Memorial in 1932, a huge Masonic landmark modeled on the ancient Lighthouse of Alexandria in Egypt, the 'Pharos'.[46]

Despite attending church services with his wife, Washington held philosophical and religious views which suggest that he, like Franklin, was a Deist. He would regularly leave services before communion, a habit which moved Reverend Dr. James

Abercrombie to compose a sermon scolding those in high positions for setting a bad example with their church attendance. Washington responded by ceasing to turn up at all. When Rev. Abercrombie was asked about Washington's religious views later in life, he simply replied: "Sir, Washington was a Deist."

THOMAS JEFFERSON

All the available evidence suggests that Thomas Jefferson was not a Freemason, although he did agree with the philosophy of the Craft and was a confirmed Deist. He created his own personal Bible from the New Testament, by omitting supernatural sections and leaving only the philosophical teachings. This unique compilation became known as the 'Jefferson Bible' – in the early 1900s approximately 2,500 copies were printed for the United States Congress.[47]

While historians point out that there is no evidence to tie Thomas Jefferson officially to any Masonic organization, it is a matter of fact that he had great sympathy for the cause. In a letter to Bishop James Madison in 1800, Jefferson relayed his thoughts on Adam Weishaupt and his Illuminati. In what amounts to a defense of both Masonry and Weishaupt's Illuminati, against the conspiracy charges laid by the writers Barruel and Robison, Jefferson's allegiances clearly lie with the Utopian and Masonic ideals rather than Church and State:

> *[Weishaupt] is among those...who believe in the indefinite perfectibility of man. He thinks he may in time be rendered so perfect that he will be able to govern himself in every circumstance so as to injure none, to do all the good he can, to leave government no occasion to exercise their powers over him...Weishaupt believes that to promote this perfection of*

the human character was the object of Jesus Christ. That his intention was simply to reinstate natural religion, and by diffusing the light of his morality, to teach us to govern ourselves. His precepts are the love of god & love of our neighbor. And by teaching innocence of conduct, he expected to place men in their natural state of liberty and equality. He says, no one ever laid a surer foundation for liberty than our grand master, Jesus of Nazareth. He believes the Free Masons were originally possessed of the true principles and objects of Christianity, and have still preserved some of them by tradition, but much disfigured.

…As Weishaupt lived under the tyranny of a despot and priests, he knew that caution was necessary even in spreading information, and the principles of pure morality. He proposed therefore to lead the Free masons to adopt this object and to make the objects of their institution the diffusion of science & virtue…

This has given an air of mystery to his views, was the foundation of his banishment, the subversion of the Masonic order, and is the colour for the ravings against him of Robison, Barruel and Morse, whose real fears are that the craft would be endangered by the spreading of information, reason and natural morality among men…if Weishaupt had written here, where no secrecy is necessary in our endeavors to render men wise and virtuous, he would not have thought of any secret machinery for that purpose.[48]

Jefferson was the primary author of the Declaration of Independence, and as well as being the third President of the United States also served at various times as Vice-President, Secretary of State and ambassador to France. During his travels to France he accompanied his good friend Benjamin Franklin to the 'Nine Sisters' Masonic lodge. Many of his closest associates and confidantes were Freemasons.

THOMAS PAINE

Thomas Paine is yet another Founding Father who held strong Deist views. Born and bred in England, Paine didn't move to the colonies until his late thirties, only a matter of years before the Declaration of Independence. He emigrated on the advice of Benjamin Franklin, whom he had met in London. Barely a year after arriving, he published the massively influential *Common Sense* on January 10th 1776, which is said to have sold more than 600,000 copies in a population of only three million. His words inspired George Washington to seek the route of independence from Great Britain, and Thomas Jefferson partly based the Declaration of Independence upon them. Paine also has the honor of being the person to suggest the name of the United States of America.[49]

This revolutionary thinker was sentenced *in absentia* in Great Britain for sedition, and despite his support for the French Revolution in his *Rights of Man,* was imprisoned and sentenced to death by the revolutionaries for arguing against the execution of Louis XVI. Miraculously, his life was spared when the executioner marked his door incorrectly.[50]

Many Americans would be surprised to know that the man who coined the name of the United States, and had such a profound impact upon its independence, had strong feelings against Christianity. In his *Age of Reason* he wrote:

> *The opinions I have advanced…are the effect of the most clear and long-established conviction that the Bible and*

the Testament are impositions upon the world, that the fall of man, the account of Jesus Christ being the Son of God, and of his dying to appease the wrath of God, and of salvation by that strange means, are all fabulous inventions, dishonorable to the wisdom and power of the Almighty; that the only true religion is Deism, by which I then meant, and mean now, the belief of one God, and an imitation of his moral character, or the practice of what are called moral virtues.[51]

There is no direct evidence that Paine was a Freemason. However, after his death an essay was published, said to be a chapter from Part III of *Age of Reason*, titled "The Origins of Freemasonry". Whatever his official status was, Paine certainly had access to information about the Craft:

The Entered Apprentice knows but little more of Masonry than the use of signs and tokens, and certain steps and words by which Masons can recognize each other without being discovered by a person who is not a Mason. The Fellow Craft is not much better instructed in Masonry, than the Entered Apprentice. It is only in the Master Mason's Lodge, that whatever knowledge remains of the origin of Masonry is preserved and concealed.[52]

Paine was an equal opportunity debunker of myth though, and wasn't afraid to point out what seemed to him to be a glaring error in the legend of Masonry:

The original institution of Masonry consisted in the foundation of the liberal arts and sciences, but more especially in Geometry, for at the building of the tower of Babel, the art and mystery of Masonry was first introduced, and from thence handed down by Euclid, a worthy and excellent mathematician of the Egyptians; and he communicated it to Hiram, the Master Mason concerned in building Solomon's Temple in Jerusalem.

Besides the absurdity of deriving Masonry from the building of Babel, where, according to the story, the confusion of languages prevented the builders understanding each other, and consequently of communicating any knowledge they had, there is a glaring contradiction in point of chronology in the account he gives.

Solomon's Temple was built and dedicated 1004 years before the Christian era; and Euclid, as may be seen in the tables of chronology, lived 277 before the same era. It was therefore impossible that Euclid could communicate any thing to Hiram, since Euclid did not live till 700 years after the time of Hiram.[53]

Paine believed that Masonry had a different origin than is stated in the myths of the Craft. He promoted his own view that Freemasonry was derived from the remnants of the Druidic religion, which was the most recent culture to bear a line of mystical knowledge which also passed through the hands of the Romans, Greeks, Egyptians and Chaldeans. And ultimately, according to Paine, Masonry was based on the worship of the heavens, and in particular, the Sun.

One of Paine's friends, the revolutionist Nicolas de Bonneville – who also counted Benjamin Franklin as a friend – was even more explicit on the Egyptian origins of modern religions and movements. In his book *De L'Esprit des Religion*, published in 1791, de Bonneville claimed that Christian religion itself stemmed from the ancient cult of Isis.[54] It has often been pointed out that statues of the Virgin Mary and baby Jesus bear a close resemblance to the Egyptian sculptures of Isis and the child Horus. Dan Brown could certainly make good mileage out of the sacred feminine angle on this issue, although the reference is perhaps a little too oblique to the central themes of his book.

Paine claimed that the veil of secrecy which Masons worked under was in order to avoid persecution by the religion which took over the worship of the Sun – Christianity:

> *The natural source of secrecy is fear. When any new religion over-runs a former religion, the professors of the new become the persecutors of the old. We see this in all instances that history brings before us...when the Christian religion over-ran the religion of the Druids in Italy, ancient Gaul, Britain, and Ireland, the Druids became the subject of persecution. This would naturally and necessarily oblige such of them as remained attached to their original religion to meet in secret, and under the strongest injunctions of secrecy...from the remains of the religion of the Druids, thus preserved, arose the institution which, to avoid the name of Druid, took that of Mason, and practiced under this new name the rites and ceremonies of Druids.*[55]

Paine's enmity against Christianity has meant that to a large extent, his role in the independence of the United States has been swept under the proverbial carpet. Theodore Roosevelt inaccurately called Paine "a dirty little atheist" (Paine did believe in a supreme being), and in 1925 Thomas Edison conceded that "if Paine had ceased his writings with *The Rights of Man* he would have been hailed today as one of the two or three outstanding figures of the Revolution...*The Age of Reason* cost him glory at the hands of his countrymen."[56]

ALEXANDER HAMILTON

Alexander Hamilton was certainly not blessed with an easy start in life. He was born in the West Indies as the illegitimate son of a struggling businessman from Scotland, James Hamilton, and Rachel Fawcett Lavien – who was at the time married to another man. His father abandoned him, and his mother died in his early teens. However, his precocious intellect and raw ambition paved the way for a meteoric rise: by the end of his teenage years, Hamilton was General George Washington's most trusted *aide-de-camp*, and a published pamphleteer of renown on the subjects of government and economics.

President George Washington appointed Hamilton as the United States' first Secretary of the Treasury, a post in which he served from 1789 until 1795. His tenure marked him as one of America's most important statesman, with some saying his financial and political genius paved the way for the United States to become the super-power it is today.

Despite his modest beginnings, Hamilton had a strong belief that only a 'chosen few' were fit to govern and that power should be centralized, once saying "ancient democracies in which the people themselves deliberated never possessed one good feature of government." His vision of the U.S. was for power to be taken away from the states and put in the hands of a central government. He also instigated the creation of the first national bank of the United States, despite intense opposition from Secretary of State Thomas Jefferson. If Dan Brown pursues a plotline involving an Illuminati-style cabal within the government, he may well point out one of Hamilton's more infamous quotes:

> *All communities divide themselves into the few and the*
> *many. The first are the rich and the well-born; the other*
> *the mass of the people...turbulent and changing, they seldom*

judge or determine right. Give therefore to the first class a
distinct, permanent share in the Government. Nothing but
a permanent body can check the imprudence of democracy.

There is some confusion as to whether Hamilton was a
Freemason. 33rd Degree Mason Henry Clausen claims Hamilton
as a 'Brother' in his book, *Masons Who Helped Shape Our Nation,* as
does Gordon S. Wood in *The Radicalism of the American Revolution.*
However, Masonic scholar Allen E. Roberts specifically states that
Hamilton was not a Mason in his respected tome, *Freemasonry in
American History.* Needless to say though, that Dan Brown may
not be fussed on the details and could well include Hamilton as a
Freemason in his book.

Hamilton's life came to a bizarre end on July 12, 1804. It
is alleged that he privately made comments questioning the
integrity of the third Vice-President of the United States, Aaron
Burr. Burr demanded an apology, but Hamilton refused – saying
he could not recall making any such remarks. A duel was set to
resolve the issue, with Burr and Hamilton coming together on a
rocky ledge in Weehawken, New Jersey – the same place where
Hamilton's son Phillip had been killed in a duel just three years
previous. Burr shot and mortally wounded Hamilton, who died
the next day.

MASONS EVERYWHERE

We have seen that a number of the Founding Fathers of the
United States were ambivalent, if not downright hostile, towards
Christianity. A strong thread of Deism runs through the ranks of
the influential personalities involved in America's independence.
But stronger still is the presence of Freemasonry. Not only were
many of the Founding Fathers initiates of the Craft, but also

numerous generals in the Continental Army, as well as other individuals who loom large in the drive for independence, such as the Frenchman Gilbert Lafayette.

This young idealistic French aristocrat took the position of Major-General in the Continental Army, with the request that he not be paid for his service, at the grand age of 19. His exemplary service for the fledgling United States earned him the respect of George Washington, whom he thereafter held as a life-long friend. Lafayette also spent time with Benjamin Franklin in Paris, where they were both members of the 'Nine Sisters' Masonic lodge – in fact, each supported an arm of the aged Voltaire as he was inducted into the influential organization. Lafayette's prominence in the Revolutionary War has led to approximately four hundred public places and streets in the United States being named after him.[57] It is said that when American troops liberated Paris in the First World War, Colonel C. E. Stanton – on behalf of the U.S. General John Perching, a 33rd Degree Freemason – stood before Lafayette's tomb on the 4th of July 1917, proclaiming "Lafayette, we are here!"[58]

One of the legendary moments in the move towards independence was the 'Boston Tea Party'. On the night of the 16th of December 1773, a group of Boston locals protesting the importation of duty-free tea from the East India Tea Company, boarded the merchant ship *Dartmouth* and dumped its entire cargo of tea into the harbor. While devoid of bloodshed, this incident marked the beginning of the Revolution, as it ignited colonial passions against the strictures and impositions of the parliament of Great Britain. What is unknown to many is that at least twelve members of the local Masonic lodge were involved in the Boston Tea Party – including the patriot Paul Revere – and at least another twelve of the participants subsequently joined it.

Another influential contributor to the drive for independence was a Jewish Freemason named Haym Solomon, who had amassed a fortune through his dealings as a banker and merchant. Solomon had a deep belief that the United States would go on to become a beacon of the world, and as such devoted not only his own fortune to the revolutionary cause, but also played a huge role in raising money from international sources – helped by his proficiency in eight languages.

Haym Solomon negotiated war aid from France and Holland, and acted as paymaster-general of the French military forces during the Revolutionary War. He is said to have loaned the fledgling government about $600,000, of which at least $400,000 was never repaid. He also financially assisted icons such as Jefferson and Madison, and was a close personal friend of George Washington.[59]

A Strange Tale

In his book *The Secret Destiny of America,* the respected esotericist Manly P. Hall recounts a bizarre piece of folklore regarding the creation of the American flag, and it bears retelling here as Dan Brown could well draw on it in *The Solomon Key.*[60] Hall says he first came across the strange tale in the 1890 book *Our Flag, or the Evolution of the Stars and Stripes,* authored by Robert Alan Campbell. It tells how the Continental Congress met in 1775 to discuss the creation of a Colonial flag; Benjamin Franklin and George Washington were two of the luminaries present.

Campbell states that the flag committee met at a house in Cambridge, Massachusetts, near where General Washington was encamped. Staying at this house was an old gentleman – referred to only as the 'Professor' – and due to space constraints Benjamin Franklin offered to share apartments with the enigmatic man. Little is known about the Professor, except that he was at least 70 years old, and he "ate no flesh, fish, nor fowl, or any green things, and drank no liquor, wine, or ale". He lived only on cereals, fruits and tea, and spent most of his time poring over ancient books and rare manuscripts.

When the Professor was introduced to the Continental Congress, Benjamin Franklin stepped forward and shook his hand. At this point, Campbell says, there was an obvious and mutual recognition between the two – perhaps indicative of a Masonic handshake or the like? In any case, after dinner Franklin exchanged a few words with Washington and the committee, and then made the curious move of asking the stranger to take part in the flag meeting.

On acceptance of the invitation, the Professor lost no time in asserting himself. He immediately recommended that the hostess be included as secretary of the committee, to increase the number of members from the inauspicious number of six to the more numerologically significant figure of seven – a suggestion that was unanimously accepted by the committee.

It is abundantly clear that this mysterious individual was well-grounded in numerology, as well as other ancient and mystical sciences such as astrology. Campbell quotes him as standing before the committee delivering this speech:

> As the sun rises from his grave in Capricorn, mounts toward his resurrection in Aries and pass onward and upward to his glorious culmination in Cancer, so will our political sun rise and continue to increase in power, in light, and in glory; and the exalted sun of summer will not have gained his full strength of heat and power in the starry Lion until our Colonial Sun will be, in its glorious exaltation, demanding a place in the governmental firmaments alongside of, coordinate with, and in no wise subordinate to, any other sun of any other nation upon earth.[61]

The Professor then recommended his design for the flag, which would allow for modification based on the upward rise of the United States. Campbell says that the committee approved this suggested design, and the flag was promptly adopted by George Washington as the standard for the Colonial Army.

DESIGNING A NATION

Although it has often been claimed that up to 50 of the 56 signatories to the Declaration of Independence were Freemasons, the 'official' number is put at between 8 and 15. While this may seem to quash the conspiracy theories, it is still a significant number, especially so when one considers that such influential personalities as Franklin and Washington were long-time Masons. Despite the modern-day belief of many that the United States is a nation built from a strong Christian base, in truth its founders were largely non-Christian and seem to have had a deep and abiding desire to create a new land where the tyrannies of religion and government – as seen in Europe – were largely kept in check.

Manly Hall's *The Secret Destiny of America* claims that the creation of the United States was the prime goal of the 'Order of the Quest', a secret society composed of intellectuals and philosophers which had survived from ancient times. Hall says that the creation of the United States was a step towards the ultimate aim of a worldwide democracy:

> *All these groups [Knights of the Holy Grail, Christian and Jewish Cabalists, Rosicrucians, the Illuminati] belong to what is called The Order of the Quest. All were searching for one and the same thing under a variety of rituals and symbols. That one thing was a perfected*

social order, Plato's commonwealth, the government of the philosopher-king.[62]

Whatever the reality, Dan Brown certainly has much to draw on for his 'hidden history' aspects in *The Solomon Key*. It is difficult to establish authoritatively whether or not secret societies guided colonial America towards a definite goal, or whether they only exercised an influence via the common philosophy shared by each of them – the ideal originally enunciated by Francis Bacon in *The New Atlantis*. It is interesting to note that the date of Independence Day, the 4th of July, is a significant date for the Knights Templar. The Knights of Solomon suffered a massive defeat at the hands of Muslim armies at the 'Horns of Hattin' on the 4th of July 1187, precipitating the loss of Jerusalem.[63] Is Dan Brown likely to reference this important event as the reason for the date of independence – signifying the rebuilding of the 'House of Solomon'?

No matter what the truth, Freemasonry most definitely played some sort of role in the creation of the new republic. Masonic historian Ronald Heaton says that the Craft was more influential than any other institution in the establishment of the United States:

> *Neither general historians nor the members of the Fraternity since the days of the first Constitutional Conventions have realized how much the United States of America owes to Freemasonry, and how great a part it played in the birth of the nation and the establishment of the landmarks of that civilization.*[64]

Incidentally, Heaton's mention of the establishment of landmarks brings us to the next possible topic in Dan Brown's *The Solomon Key*: the Masonic architecture of Washington, D.C.

CHAPTER 5

STRANGE CONSTRUCTIONS

As we saw at the start of the last chapter, the beginning of construction work in the United States capital was heavily flavored with Masonic overtones. With local lodges presiding over cornerstone ceremonies, and the President himself being a Freemason, it would appear that the building of Washington, D.C. may have been strongly influenced by the culture of the Craft. This is an idea that is worth a closer look: in the news stories that emerged in early November 2004 concerning the disclosure of the title of *The Solomon Key*, there were further hints about the content of the book:

> *In first discussing the subject of the book last spring, Brown mentioned that the architecture of Washington is rich in symbolism, something that he is using in the novel.*[65]

This is no great surprise – both of Brown's Robert Langdon novels used the art and architecture of well-known cities as 'props' for their plot. In *Angels and Demons* Langdon follows the 'Way of Light' marked by the sculptures of Bernini, with many other references to the architecture of Rome spread throughout the book. In *The Da Vinci Code,* Brown uses the art of the Renaissance master Leonardo da Vinci, as well as some of the esoteric themes in Parisian architecture (and Rosslyn towards the end of the book).

We should therefore take a closer look at the history and architecture of Washington, D.C., with an eye to discerning which details are most likely to be mentioned by Dan Brown in *The Solomon Key.* One book in particular that may be of help is *The Secret Architecture of Our Nation's Capital,* by David Ovason. Also of note is *Talisman,* by Graham Hancock and Robert Bauval. We will also consult miscellaneous sources regarding specific monuments in the capital. Please note that various maps of the city are available in the Appendix.

Designing History

The site of Washington, D.C. was selected during a dinner between Thomas Jefferson and Alexander Hamilton, with Jefferson agreeing to support Hamilton's federal financial plans in exchange for land dedicated to a capital. The states of Virginia and Maryland donated the necessary land, and in 1790 the site was designated as the District of Columbia, with the capital taking its name from George Washington.

The city plan was originally designed by the Frenchman Pierre Charles l'Enfant, who had served in the Revolutionary War after arriving with Lafayette. David Ovason claims that l'Enfant was a Freemason, although he cites unpublished documents as his basis for this assertion. Due to personality conflicts, l'Enfant was dismissed from his position early on in the project. The emotional Frenchman took his design drawings with him when he left, but the plan was still reproduced reasonably faithfully from the memory of those who continued with the project. An astronomer and surveyor, Andrew Ellicott, took over from l'Enfant, with both Jefferson and Washington contributing ideas.

Washington, D.C. is divided into four quadrants, marked by the cardinal directions, with the center point being the Capitol building. However, as the Capitol is not at the center of the district, the quadrants are unequal in size. L'Enfant's plan for Washington, D.C. includes many diagonal avenues which are named after the states, probably the most famous of which is Pennsylvania Avenue which connects the White House and the Capitol. In the original plan, the Capitol, the White House and the Washington Monument form a right-angled triangle.

As a side note, the White House used to be called the Presidential Mansion, until it was burned by the British during a raid in 1814 – along with the Capitol and the bridge across the Potomac. As a consequence, white paint was used to disguise the blackened walls, and from that point on it was referred to as the White House.

WASHINGTON AND THE SACRED FEMININE

The fact that Dan Brown has cited the architecture of Washington, D.C. as being important to his next book is not the only reason to reference *The Secret Architecture of Our Nation's Capital*. For though Ovason discusses many aspects of the design of the city and of specific monuments and architecture in his book, there is one other part of his research that ties him to the 'symbology' of Dan Brown. Ovason sees the capital of the United States as being founded by Masons, and devoted to the goddess principle – be it Isis, Demeter, or the Virgin.

Ovason's *Secret Architecture* analyzes some twenty zodiacs found in Washington, D.C., as well as the astrological charts for important days in the construction of the capital:

> *The imagery of Virgo as ruler of Washington, D.C. is reflected in the considerable number of Zodiacs and lapidary symbols which grace the city. The Virgoan connection has also been emphasized in a number of foundation charts which are of fundamental importance to Washington, D.C.*[66]

While some Freemasons have criticized what they see as Ovason's 'mumbo-jumbo' approach in finding significance in astrological charts, others have rightly pointed out that there is a definite history of Freemasons casting horoscopes before the commencement of construction activities. For example, in *Talisman*, Graham Hancock and Robert Bauval point out that, after the devastation of the Great Fire of London in 1666, the early Mason Elias Ashmole was consulted about the most favorable dates for the laying of the cornerstones of important buildings.[67]

Some, including Ovason, have also raised the famous Craft image of the 'Monument to a Master Mason' as evidence that the 'sacred feminine' is a vital part of the Masonic tradition. It portrays a virgin standing above a broken column, with a sprig of acacia in her hand, and Father Time standing behind her, sometimes touching her hair. However, some have debunked this claim, with one Masonic source refuting Ovason with the following words:

> *Ovason's theory stands or falls on the assumption...that freemasons held similar views about astrology that he does, and that Freemasonry places any significance in Virgo...his*

Monument to a Master Mason

assumptions are unproven and his theory fails to pass any reasonable examination.[68]

However, another area of Ovason's research regarding the geometry of Washington, D.C. is also of great interest. He points out a fascinating painting of the Washington family, by Edward Savage, which shows three members of the family discretely outlining a triangular area on a map of Washington with disguised hand placement[69]. Is this triangle indicating a certain location within the capital, or is it a sly 'nod of the

Washington Family Portrait, by Edward Savage

head' to Craft members via the outline of a Masonic compass (note the looped fingers at the top of the 'triangle')? Note too that in this picture we find Washingon's grandson holding a Masonic compass above a globe, as well as a checkerboard floor – both distinctly Masonic motifs. As this painting hangs in the National Gallery of Art in Washington, D.C., we may see Robert Langdon dropping in for a look.

STREETS AND SYMBOLS

Many conspiracy theorists have pointed out other specific geometry which they say was also a part of the original design of the capital. Some see the Masonic square and compass design in l'Enfant's diagonal street plans – the Capitol being the top of the compass with each leg leading to the White House and the Jefferson Memorial. Others have pointed out a 'Satanic' upside-down pentagram which can be traced to the north of the White House, with the lowest point of the symbol beginning at the Presidential residence.

On a slightly more orthodox note, Michael Baigent and Richard Leigh make quick mention of the street plan in *The Temple and the Lodge*. All that they say is that the Capitol and the White House were each focal points of an "elaborate geometry governing the layout" of Washington, D.C. They also mention that the original design of l'Enfant was modified by Washington and Jefferson to produce octagonal patterns reminiscent of the insignia cross of the Knights Templar.

Authors Graham Hancock and Robert Bauval also mention the possibility of an intentional alignment along Pennsylvania Avenue, between the White House and the site of the Capitol building (Jenkins Hill), with the rising of the brightest star in the sky, Sirius. The heliacal rising of Sirius was of great importance to the ancient Egyptians, as it signified their New Year. The star was also closely associated with the great goddess of ancient Egypt, Isis – yet another tie-in to the sacred feminine. Hancock and Bauval point out that any observer looking along Pennsylvania Avenue at dawn in 1793 would have seen Sirius 'hovering' over the proposed site of the Capitol, a feature they believe could not have been missed by individuals like the astronomer Ellicott:

> *That such portentous astral symbolism could have gone unnoticed by the group of important Freemasons and astronomers who planned Washington and decided the locations of its principal structures, seems most unlikely.*[70]

In *Talisman*, Hancock and Bauval also suggest that the street-plan of Washington, D.C. deliberately incorporates the

Kabbalistic 'Tree of Life' symbol (although truthfully, one could just as easily see a Christian Cross). They see the Capitol building as the 'head' of the esoteric symbol (designated as 'Kether'), with the Tree of Life unfolding to the west. One of the major landmarks which they see sitting within this symbol, at a point corresponding to the Kabbalistic sephirah of 'Tipheret', is the gigantic obelisk of the Washington Monument.[71] Whether or not this correspondence was planned, it is worth looking more closely at this monument, modeled on the impressive landmarks of ancient Egypt.

THE WASHINGTON MONUMENT

The cornerstone of the Washington Monument, an eleven tonne block of Maryland marble, was formally laid by Grandmaster Benjamin B. French of the Grand Lodge of Free and Accepted Masons of the District of Columbia on Sunday July 4th, 1848. He is said to have worn George Washington's Masonic apron and sash, and held the same Mason's gavel that Washington had used when laying the cornerstone of the U.S. Capitol on September 18th, 1793.[72]

The Washington Monument was first conceived of in 1799, eight days after the death of Washington. It was proposed that "a Marble monument be erected by the United States in the Capitol, at the City of Washington, and that the family of George Washington be requested to permit his body to be to be deposited under it."[73] However, the refusal of the Washington family to move the former President's body meant that the project was continually shelved.

Public displeasure at the failure of the government to create a lasting memorial for Washington finally resulted in the creation of the Washington National Monument Society, which set about raising the funds necessary through private sources. Congress set aside an area of land for the monument, and it was decided to build it at a point which aligned due south of the White House and due west of the Capitol – incidentally, a location that the original designer of Washington, D.C., Pierre l'Enfant, had marked out for a monument to Washington. However, unsuitable ground meant that it was shifted 100 yards to the south-east of this point, somewhat spoiling the alignment.

The monument was originally planned as an obelisk 600 feet in height, with a flat apex surmounted by a 'blazing 5-pointed star' – a distinctly Masonic symbol. The base of the monument was planned to have a surrounding 'pantheon' of marble columns 100 feet high. However, shortly after the beginning of construction the planned height was reduced to 500 feet, and a pyramidion was substituted for the blazing star. Then, when the Society began to run short on resources, a plan was instituted whereby other states and countries could contribute blocks of marble (or other durable stones) to the project from their own soil.

This resulted in one of the more famous incidents in the history of the Washington Monument. The Vatican, led by Pope Pius IX, contributed a block of historic marble from the Temple of Concord in Rome, approximately 3 feet long, 10 inches thick and 18 inches high. However, the xenophobic and anti-Catholic 'American Party' (also popularly known as the 'Know-Nothings') took umbrage with the outside contribution, and vowed that the stone would never become a part of the Washington Monument.

On March 6th 1854 the "Pope's Stone", as it has come to be known, was stolen. A $100 reward was posted for its return, but the stone was never recovered. The most popular theory is that it was dumped into the nearby Potomac River, although another theory states that it was buried at the intersection of two streets in Washington, D.C. Considering that the two Robert Langdon

Washington Monument with White House in Background

novels so far have involved the Vatican, Dan Brown may well be tempted to read something into this minor mystery for the sake of the plot of *The Solomon Key*.

Indeed, we can predict with reasonable confidence that Dan Brown will incorporate the Washington Monument into *The Solomon Key* in some manner, and not just because of its inherent Egyptian symbolism and importance to the landscape of the capital. For in *The Da Vinci Code*, Brown inexplicably measures the length of the Grand Gallery in the Louvre as "three Washington Monuments laid end to end." Considering that he has been researching these books somewhat concurrently, this may be a telling slip of the tongue.

Scottish Rite Supreme Council

Another location that may be used in *The Solomon Key* is the headquarters of the 'Mother Supreme Council' of 33rd Degree Masonry (Southern Jurisdiction of the Scottish Rite), which is located at 1733 16th Street NW in Washington, D.C. Modeled on the mausoleum of Helicarnassus, this building – known as the 'House of the Temple' – was designed in 1911 by the famous architect John Russell Pope and is covered in Egyptian symbols such as the Sphinx, the Ankh and the Uraeus.[74]

David Ovason points out that the great tower which tops the House of the Temple is a replica of the truncated pyramid which famously decorates the reverse side of the Great Seal of the United States – the Illuminati symbol of *Angels and Demons* – right down to the detail of being constructed out of 13 courses of stonework.[75] The building had two architects: with Pope not being a Freemason, a 32nd Degree Mason named Elliott Woods was also employed to work on the building. Woods' Masonic expertise was obviously necessary for the correct interior design

Scottish Rite "House of the Temple" (© J. Alison)

of the Masonic temple. Ovason notes that Pope's original design had many more than 13 courses for the pyramid, but it is not known who made the decision to modify the plan.

In *Angels and Demons* Dan Brown focused on the many sculptures by Bernini around the ancient city of Rome. He may be tempted to reference John Russell Pope in the same way, as Pope also designed many other architectural masterpieces around Washington, D.C., including the Jefferson Memorial, the National Archives, and National Gallery of Art.

ROSE-LINE OF WASHINGTON?

Incidentally, there is an oblique relationship between the location of the House of the Temple and *The Da Vinci Code* which Dan Brown may well incorporate into *The Solomon Key*. In *The Da Vinci Code*, Dan Brown remarked about the 'Rose-Line' and the meridian of Paris which passes through St Sulpice.

Dr Steven Mizrach, an anthropologist at Florida International University and a respected researcher of the Priory of Sion mystery, points out that – like Paris – the U.S. capital once had its own meridian:

> *Apparently, DC was originally designed so that 16th street would be its original north-south meridian – and this meridian was going to be the "zero meridian" of the United States. After Greenwich was made the international meridian, DC and Paris both renounced their claims. Today, DC uses Capitol Street as its N-S axis, but certain monuments, especially those in Meridian Hill Park, point to the older axis.*[76]

The Scottish Rite's 'House of the Temple' is also located on 16th street. A book titled *The Jefferson Stone – Demarcation of the First Meridian of the United States*, by Silvio A. Bedini, tells how Thomas Jefferson was a driving force behind the effort to establish a prime meridian in America. This meridian was designated as passing through the mid-point of the White House. A plaque commemorating this abandoned proposal still stands today at the upper entrance to Meridian Hill Park, entered from 16th street, on the site of a previous marker established in 1816.[77]

THE PENTAGON

The Pentagon is worthy of a mention purely on the basis of its geometric construction. The five-sided shape of the building is a notable geometric figure, and also has the quality of neatly enclosing the 'magical' symbol of the pentagram (five-pointed star). Dan Brown showed his affinity for the 'Golden Section' within the pentagram in *The Da Vinci Code*, so we could well expect a monologue regarding the headquarters of the U.S. military in *The Solomon Key*. The pentagram symbol was first found in ancient Egypt, as a hieroglyph denoting 'star' (and by relation, the heavens).

It is said that the distinctive shape of the building arose from the problematic shape of the location originally proposed as the building site. However, a different location was later chosen, which raises the question of why the strange design was retained when the new site had none of the restrictions of the original. Another reason given for the shape of the building is that it maximizes work efficiency by making every office accessible within a few minutes walk...although we might ask why a high-rise with elevators could not have achieved the same result. In any case, construction of the building began in July 1941.

Graham Hancock and Robert Bauval point out in *Talisman* that President Franklin Delano Roosevelt, who took control of the planning of the building, was raised as a Master Freemason in 1911 and in 1929 became a 32nd Degree Scottish Rite Mason. He should therefore have been quite aware of one of Scottish Rite Masonry's key works, *Morals and Dogma* by Albert Pike, which associates the pentagon shape with the Masonic Blazing Star symbol. [78]

George Washington Masonic Memorial

Located in the independent city of Alexandria in Virginia, some six miles south of Washington, D.C., is the George Washington National Masonic Memorial (see image p. 62). The idea of erecting a Masonic memorial to George Washington was formulated by several members of Alexandria–Washington Lodge No. 22, which had lost numerous historical treasures in a series of fires. The Lodge decided to construct a fire-proof building to house the remaining Washington memorabilia given to them by the Washington family.

Construction of the Memorial was financed entirely by the voluntary contributions from members of the Masonic Fraternity. As such, it is considered to belong to all Freemasons in the United States, regardless of their 'branch' affiliation. The cornerstone was laid on November 1st, 1923, but construction proceeded only as funds became available. Thus, the Memorial was not dedicated until May 12th, 1932 – a moment described as "one of the most important and exciting events in the history of American Freemasonry."

Despite not actually being a part of Washington, D.C., the Memorial would certainly be a suitable location for *The Solomon Key*: the building is a spectacular landmark standing 333 feet in height, and is said to have been modeled on the ancient Pharos lighthouse of Alexandria in Egypt (one of the Seven Wonders of the Ancient World). Visitors enter the building via 'Memorial Hall' on the second floor, and are greeted by a massive sculpture of George Washington wearing his Masonic apron. Might we see Robert Langdon visiting the George Washington Museum which is housed on the fourth floor, and which contains historic memorabilia related to both Masonry and the nation's first President? Or perhaps the library on the sixth floor which contains some 20,000 books on the Craft?

However, two of the levels above the library are the most likely settings for *The Solomon Key*. On the seventh floor can be found a 'replica' of the crypt beneath King Solomon's Temple – the perfect scene for discovering some secret relating to Solomon. And on the ninth (and uppermost) floor of the Memorial is a reconstruction of the Throne Room of King Solomon's Temple. This level is surrounded by an observation deck, which provides a panoramic view of the metropolitan Washington area.

Writing in the *Scottish Rite Journal* (Feb. 2001), 33rd Degree Mason George D. Seghers described the mission of the George Washington Masonic National Memorial Association:

> *Our task today is not only to preserve the memory and legacy of George Washington but also to preserve, promote, and perpetuate the Masonic beliefs and ideals upon which this great nation was founded.*

Seghers' words echo the basic plotline of *The Solomon Key*: that the United States was founded upon, and continues to be influenced by, the ideals of Freemasonry. Between the Masonic books and relics housed there, and the 'copies' of King Solomon's Temple which can be found on the higher floors, the George Washington Masonic Memorial certainly provides a worthy setting for Brown's upcoming novel.

An Endless List

There are numerous other locations in Washington, D.C. which Dan Brown could easily insert into the plot of *The Solomon Key*. There are a curious number of areas in the capital named after Egyptian place names, such as Alexandria. There are also various 'coincidences' which could be called on as being of historical interest: for example, the White House cornerstone ceremony was held on October 13th, the Templars' day of infamy.

Naturally enough, the United States capital is filled with monuments – some of which are well-known, some of which are less well-known but display esoteric symbolism. For instance, the headquarters of the Internal Revenue Service (I.R.S.) has some distinctive sculptures surrounding it such as a small pyramid at its entrance, as well as a hand pointing a finger to the heavens

– a gesture which receives plenty of attention in Picknett and Prince's book *The Templar Revelation* as an 'insignia' of Leonardo Da Vinci. The more public Capitol building has its own specific points of interest (see Ovason's book for a full run-down), and was the creation of the architect and Freemason Benjamin Latrobe.

Other nearby areas could easily become part of the plot as well, such as C.I.A. headquarters in Langley, Virginia, which houses the Kryptos sculpture that we mentioned earlier. The numerous intelligence and defense agencies in the area offer up plenty of choices for a Dan Brown plotline. And, considering the jet-setting nature of Robert Langdon in *The Da Vinci Code*, there is also the possibility of visits to other monuments around the nation which have Masonic ties, such as the Statue of Liberty.

Clearly, we cannot list every possible location which may appear in *The Solomon Key* – we haven't even discussed such architectural and cultural icons as the White House and the many museums of the Smithsonian Institute. In fact the whole mall area between the Capitol and the Washington Monument is jammed full of worthy settings. However, the above-mentioned locales should at least provide some of the key settings and topics for the book.

Let's finish with a quick run-down of some of the more obscure locations which might figure in *The Solomon Key*, due to their similarity with settings in the previous Robert Langdon books:

- The bronze bas-relief images of the Great Seal set into the marble pavement of Freedom Plaza, similar to Bernini's *West Ponente* which featured in *Angels and Demons* (the 'Air' marker).

- The Department of Commerce building, in which David Ovason correlates the Mining, Fisheries, Commerce and Aeronautics tympana with the elements Earth, Water, Fire and Air – a central theme of *Angels and Demons*.

- A memorial statue to assassinated President James Garfield near the Capitol building which features Masonic symbolism.

- A marble sculpture within the Capitol building named *The Car of History*, carved by Carlo Franzoni in 1819, which features a goddess in a chariot surrounded by astrological symbolism.

- *Freedom*, the 20-foot-high statue of a goddess which surmounts the dome of the Capitol building, sculpted by Freemason Thomas Crawford.

- The 'Federal Triangle' on the map of Washington, D.C., constructed by joining the White House, Capitol, and planned site of the Washington Monument. Ovason correlates these points with the stars Regulus, Spica and Arcturus, which form a triangle in the sky enclosing the constellation of Virgo.

These are just a few of the possibilities – we'll leave it to Dan Brown to surprise us with the rest. If you'd like more detailed information on the esoteric architecture of Washington, D.C., take a look at David Ovason's book. At this point though, we'll leave this subject and begin delving into Masonic conspiracy theories, and the strange symbolism on the Great Seal of the United States.

CHAPTER 6

A MASONIC CONSPIRACY?

The Great Seal of the United States has probably been the subject of more conspiracy theories than any other national symbol. The two-sided Seal depicts an Eagle on its 'front', holding both arrows and olive branches. On the reverse side we find the more controversial image, a truncated pyramid with an 'All-Seeing Eye' as its pyramidion – a symbol that many have associated with a conspiracy headed by the group called 'the Illuminati'.

The 'Da Vinci Challenge' on Dan Brown's website explicitly mentions the mysterious symbolism found on the Great Seal of the United States as being related to *The Solomon Key*. It also made an appearance in *Angels and Demons,* the first Robert Langdon book, and Dan Brown has discussed it during interviews. As such, it is obviously worth a more detailed look, as are Dan Brown's words on the subject.

Another book by the author David Ovason might be worth consulting on this topic. *The Secret Symbols of the Dollar Bill* provides comprehensive information about the symbolism of the Seal and its later incorporation into the United States dollar bill. The esoteric author Manly Hall also discusses the Great Seal in some of his work, so we'll see what he has to say as well. Lastly, we'll finish off with a look at the possibility that the emblem encapsulates the idea of Francis Bacon's 'New Atlantis', and that it may still be a goal of some of those in power today – more than two hundred years after the Declaration of Independence.

History of the Great Seal

Before adjourning on the ground-breaking day of July 4, 1776, the Continental Congress passed a resolution that a committee be formed to design a seal for the newly independent United States. The members of that committee were Benjamin Franklin, John Adams and Thomas Jefferson – three of the five men who worked on the Declaration of Independence, two of whom would go on to become President. However, it would take another six years before the Great Seal of the United States came into being, with two more committees and fourteen men eventually employed to establish the icon.

The first committee of Franklin, Adams and Jefferson initially worked on Biblical and classical themes, including the 'Children of Israel in the Wilderness'[79], but with little success. They then employed the talents of French portrait artist, Pierre Eugene du Simitiere, who had some experience in designing seals. However, the du Simitiere-influenced design was rejected by Congress on August 20th 1776, although a couple of the features later became a part of the official seal – the infamous Eye of Providence within a triangle, and the motto *E Pluribus Unum*.[80]

Four years later, a second committee was appointed to take over the design of the Great Seal. They asked Francis Hopkinson, who had contributed to the design of both the American flag and the great seal of the State of New Jersey, to serve as consultant on the project. However, Congress rejected this design as well.

Like the previous effort though, some features were retained in later designs – the 13 red and white stripes on the shield held by the eagle, the constellation of 13 six-pointed stars, and the olive branch as a symbol of peace.[81]

In May 1782, Congress appointed a third committee to continue with the design. This they did with maximum efficiency – by promptly assigning the job to a lawyer from Philadelphia named William Barton. Barton added the important figure of the eagle to the design, and also designed the enigmatic pyramid found on the reverse of the seal, combining it with the first committee's Eye of Providence. Barton worked quickly, and the third committee turned in its report to Congress just five days after being appointed.

However, the ever-fussy Congress was still not satisfied, and the project became the responsibility of Charles Thomson, Secretary of Congress. Though not a great artist, Thomson was able to incorporate the various features into an acceptable design, while also adding the Latin mottoes *Annuit Coeptis* and *Novus Ordo Seclorum* to the reverse of the seal. He then employed Barton again to finish the job artistically, and finally the Great Seal of the United States was accepted by Congress on June 20th 1782.

The Obverse of the Seal

The obverse side of the Great Seal today depicts a Bald Eagle with outstretched wings. In its left claw it holds a bundle of arrows, while in the right we find an olive branch – the head of the eagle is turned to its right, which is said to indicate that the United States favors peace, although it is always prepared to make war if necessary. Though the United States does not have an official coat-of-arms, the eagle image is often used in its place.

Manly Hall, in *The Secret Teachings of All Ages*, claims that the bird portrayed on the original seal was not in fact an eagle, but the mythological phoenix. He based this claim on the small tuft of feathers rising from the back of its head, similar to Egyptian depictions of the Phoenix. Hall says:

> In the Mysteries it was customary to refer to initiates as 'phoenixes' or 'men who had been born again'...born into a consciousness of the spiritual world.[82]

According to Manly Hall, the "hand of the Mysteries" was involved in the founding of the United States, and the Great Seal acts as its signature. He does admit though that only a student of symbolism is fit to see through the subterfuge of the modern-day claim that the bird is an eagle. Hall is at the very least partly correct with his claim, because one of the

Obverse of the Great Seal

early designs – by William Barton – clearly shows a phoenix sitting upon its characteristic nest of flames. We'll continue to call it an eagle, for the sake of simplicity, but Hall's claims are worth remembering.

The eagle holds in its beak a banner which reads *E Pluribus Unum*, meaning 'Out of many, One'. This is a reference to the joining of the original thirteen colonies into the United States of America – fittingly, there are thirteen letters in the phrase itself. But this is probably more than a coincidence, for the number thirteen is in fact found throughout the Great Seal: there are thirteen arrows in the eagle's left claw, the shield is made up of thirteen stripes, and above the eagle there are thirteen stars. It should be noted that thirteen is also a 'power number' in Freemasonry.

One point noted by conspiracy theorists is that the thirteen stars above the head of the eagle are arranged to form the 'Seal of Solomon', a hexagram also known as the 'Star of David'. This often leads to fanciful accusations of a Jewish conspiracy, although some researchers have suggested that the financier Haym Solomon may have been involved in the placement of this 'constellation'. Interestingly, the individual stars in the hexagram design were originally hexagrams themselves, but were changed into pentagrams at some point.[83]

We have already noted the symbolism of the pentagram, but there is one additional side-note worthy of mention. In *The Secret Symbols of the Dollar Bill,* David Ovason raises the possibility that the earliest official use of the five-pointed star in North America may have been at the request of none other than Francis Bacon.[84]

THE REVERSE OF THE SEAL

If the obverse of the Great Seal raises some eyebrows, the reverse side is a veritable feast for the conspiracy theorist. The primary motif on the back side of the seal is an unfinished pyramid consisting of thirteen courses of masonry. Some say the image is very similar to the pyramids of Central America. It is more likely though, that it is a simplistic illustration of the Great Pyramid of Giza, in Egypt. This wonder of the ancient world, which stands some 450 feet in height, is also missing its capstone. It consists of substantially more than thirteen courses of masonry though!

At the base of the pyramid the year 1776 is inscribed in Roman numerals. This is said to refer to the date of the Declaration of Independence of the United States. However, to conspiracy theorists the date has a second meaning, for on May 1st 1776 Adam Weishaupt formed the Order of the Bavarian Illuminati. This is just one piece of evidence that is said to point to the seal being an emblem of the Illuminati brotherhood.

Above the truncated pyramid hovers the so-called 'Eye of Providence', contained within a triangle. Brown says this particular feature is "symbolic of the Illuminati's desire to bring about 'enlightened change' from the myth of religion to the truth of science." However, others – funnily enough, Masons included – have said the combination of pyramid and all-seeing eye was not a motif of Freemasonry at the time, and that the association probably arose in 1884 when Harvard professor, Eliot Norton, wrote that the emblem was...

...practically incapable of effective treatment; it can hardly, (however artistically treated by the designer), look otherwise than as a dull emblem of a Masonic fraternity.[85]

Masonic Apron of George Washington

The claim that Norton provided the Masonic context of the Great Seal design is certainly mistaken, if not disingenuous. David Ovason points out numerous rebuttals – one of the earliest uses of the all-seeing eye was by Freemason and founder of the Royal Society, Robert Moray.[86] The personal seal of Moray, which can be found on his private correspondence, has a radiant eye at its center – and incidentally also features a five-pointed star. The pyramid was a common image in early 18th century lodges, and a Lodge Summons dated 1757, to the Philadelphia Ancient Lodge No. 2 clearly portrays the all-seeing eye.

Moreover, there are more direct links between the 'all-seeing eye' and the Founding Fathers. As Ovason points out in *The Secret Architecture of Our Nation's Capital*, Benjamin Franklin would almost certainly have been conversant with the work of the French Freemason Theodore Tschoudy, who equated French Freemasonry with a blazing five-pointed star carrying within it the all-seeing eye.[87] And if anybody still has any doubt that the Founding Fathers were 'in' on the Masonic symbolism of the all-seeing eye, I would gently direct them to look at the Masonic apron of Brother George Washington on the previous page.

Two mottoes appear on the reverse side of the seal. Across the top of the Great Seal we see the Latin phrase *Annuit Coeptis*, which is generally translated as 'He has favored our undertaking'. Around the bottom a separate phrase is inscribed, *Novus Ordo Seclorum*, taken to mean 'a new order of the ages'. Note that two of the three mottoes on the Great Seal are made up of thirteen letters. Beyond that fact though, there is also an eye-opening geometrical code to be found in the two mottoes written on the reverse of the Great Seal, although it is not known whether it was put there on purpose or was simply a bizarre coincidence.

Those with sharp eyes have found that a hexagram, or 'Seal of Solomon', can be constructed overlaying this side of the seal. If one circles the 'A' in 'Annuit', the 's' in 'Coeptis', the 'N' in 'Novus', the final 'o' in 'Ordo' and the 'm' in 'Seclorum', we have five quite equidistant points, apart from one large gap. It is quite obvious that making another circle at the top of the 'All-seeing eye' triangle will give six points from which a hexagram can be constructed. While the ability to fit a hexagram so neatly on the seal is interesting enough, the real excitement comes when we look at the letters we circled to do so – A, S, N, O and M. Anyone with a degree of skill in constructing anagrams will see that there is one very relevant possibility from this set of letters – the word MASON.

One last point while we are discussing the Latin mottoes: we should also note that there is some confusion on the meaning of the Latin word *seclorum* – the orthodox opinion is that the word originated with the classical poet Virgil, in which context it meant 'for all time', or 'for the ages'. However, others – including Dan Brown – have tied the word to the modern 'secular', and its opposition to 'religious'. In Brown's own words, *Novus Ordo Seclorum* is a "clear call to the secular or non-religious." This theme ties in well with the Rosicrucian tradition running through Francis Bacon and the subsequent 'Royal Society', right up to Benjamin Franklin, Thomas Jefferson and Thomas Paine – who were

MASON Hexagram on the Great Seal

all scientists and Deists. The question is: has this tradition survived into modern times?

ANTI-CHRIST SUPERSTAR

Any secret society, by its very nature, is bound to be the subject of rumor and accusations. Add to that any whiff of magical or hermetic thinking and those of the 'orthodox' point of view are sure to feel threatened. Masonry is no different: as early as 1698, almost two decades before the 'official' beginnings of Freemasonry, we find pamphlets warning of the danger of the Craft:

> For this devilish sect are Meeters in secret which swere against all without their Following. They are the Anti-Christ which was to come leading them from Fear of God. For how should they meet in secret places and with secret Signs taking care that none observe them to do the Work of God; are not these the Ways of Evil-dom? [88]

The Papal Bulls condemning Freemasonry in the mid-18th Century would only have served to fuel the conspiratorial fires in the public consciousness. Then, at the end of the 18th Century, the 'overthrow' of the British in the American colonies and the monarchy in France – at least partly under the influence of known Masons – would have created an inferno. In some quarters, the execution of the King of France was seen as a revenge killing by the Templars on behalf of their last master, Jacques de Molay.

A number of books appeared immediately after the French Revolution began, accusing Freemasons of masterminding the action. Then, in 1797, came arguably the most influential 'anti-Masonry' book of the past two centuries: *Mémoires pour servir à l'histoire du jacobinisme*, by Abbe Augustin de Barruel. Educated by the Jesuits, Barruel claimed to have been initiated as a Master Mason, but did not make a vow of secrecy and thus felt he could warn the public of the alleged dangers of the Craft. On the other hand, some might be tempted to see the hand of the Jesuit order in this book's attack on Freemasonry.

At the same time in Scotland, a Professor of Natural Philosophy at the University of Edinburgh began his own book on the 'Masonic conspiracy'. John Robison had been initiated as a Mason in the early 1770s, but had lost interest soon after and discontinued his membership. However, the events of the following two decades led him to re-examine the aspirations of his former brethren, and as a result he published a book titled *Proofs of a Conspiracy against all the Religions and Governments of Europe, Carried on in the Secret Meetings of Freemasons, Illuminati, and Reading Societies*. Much of the material used today by conspiracy theorists derives from the works of Barruel and Robison, even though the majority of the content of these books appears to be no more than innuendo and rumor.

The threat of an Illuminati conspiracy was present in the minds of many people around the world, and even George Washington was appraised of this alleged conspiracy. In reply to a letter he had received regarding Robison's book, Washington defended Freemasonry – although he also appears to have mispresented his own involvement with Masonic lodges:

> *I have heard much of the nefarious, and dangerous plan, and doctrines of the Illuminati, but never saw the Book until you were pleased to send it to me…The fact is, I preside over [no English Lodges], nor have I been in one more than once or twice, within the last thirty years. I believe*

*notwithstanding, that none of the Lodges in this Country
are contaminated with the principles ascribed to the Society
of the Illuminati.*

In a second letter, Washington continues to talk about the
reputation of the Illuminati:

*It was not my intention to doubt that, the Doctrines of
the Illuminati, and principles of Jacobinism had not
spread in the United States. On the contrary, no one is
more truly satisfied of this fact than I am.*

*The idea that I meant to convey, was, that I did not believe
that the Lodges of Free Masons in this Country had, as
Societies, endeavoured to propagate the diabolical tenets of
the first, or pernicious principles of the latter (if they are
susceptible of seperation). That Individuals of them may
have done it, or that the founder, or instrument employed
to found, the Democratic Societies in the United States,
may have had these objects; and actually had a seperation
of the People from their Government in view, is too evident
to be questioned.*

Washington's letters are a graphic illustration of the
conspiratorial fever that Barruel and Robison's books had
engendered. Fearful monarchies across Europe clamped down
on secret societies and fraternities to minimize the possibility
of being the 'next France'. Meanwhile, in the United States, a
great controversy would erupt within three decades which would
change the face of Freemasonry.

In 1826, a man by the name of William Morgan came into
dispute with Masonic lodges in the New York area. As revenge, he
began work on an exposé of the Craft, which caused mayhem in

the local Freemasonry community. All of a sudden, on September 19th 1826, William Morgan disappeared. Although research has shown that Morgan was probably 'resettled' in Canada by Masons with some cash and a warning to never come back, there are still many who believe that he was murdered for his threat to reveal the Craft's secrets.

If the Morgan affair came to dominate anti-Masonry in the 19th Century, then the 20th Century can boast its own defining moment. Curiously enough, it features the re-emergence of the esoteric figures on the Great Seal. In 1934 the United States Secretary of Agriculture, Henry Wallace, became interested in the mysterious iconography of the seal. There is a good reason for this, as Wallace was a mystically oriented Freemason initiated to the 32nd Degree in the Scottish Rite, affiliated with the District of Columbia Scottish Rite body.[89]

Wallace decided to show the seal to President Franklin Roosevelt. Wallace described the meeting:

> *Roosevelt…was first struck with the representation of the all-seeing eye – a Masonic representation of the Great Architect of the Universe. Next, he was impressed with the idea that the foundation for the new order of the ages had been laid in 1776 but that it would be completed only under the eye of the Great Architect. Roosevelt, like myself, was a 32nd Degree Mason. He suggested that the Seal be put on the dollar bill.*[90]

This would not prove to be a difficult task, as the Secretary of the Treasury at the time, Henry Morgenthau, was also a Freemason.[91] Since that time though, this controversial move has been at the center of Masonic conspiracy allegations. Henry Wallace went on to become Vice-President of the United States. Roosevelt, the 32nd President and a 32nd degree Mason,

Great Seal on the Dollar Bill

was succeeded by Harry Truman, the 33rd President and a 33rd degree Freemason.[92]

Wallace was also a devout fundamentalist Christian, and was described by his biographer as having a Messianic complex, as well as the strong belief that God had ordained America to lead the world.[93] He also used the familiar concept of a 'New World Order', a subject sure to raise alarm bells with conspiracy theorists. Lynn Picknett and Clive Prince – authors of Dan Brown favourite *The Templar Revelation* – point out in their book *The Stargate Conspiracy* that Wallace said in 1934:

> It will take a more definite recognition of the Grand Architect of the Universe before the apex stone is finally fitted into place and this nation in the full strength of its power is in position to assume leadership among the nations in inaugurating 'the new order of the ages'.[94]

Around the same time that Wallace made this statement, the famous psychic healer Edward Cayce had this to say in one of his 'readings':

*Americanism with the universal thought that is expressed
and manifest in the Brotherhood of man into group thought,
as expressed by the Masonic order, will be the eventual rule
in the settlement of affairs in the world.*[95]

In a government-commissioned report of 1973, Freemasonry
is recommended as a tonic to the diverse changes occurring in
American society. The author of the report, Willis Harman, later
wrote about the Great Seal:

*The specific symbols associated with the nation's birth
have an additional significance. It is under these symbols,
principle and goals, properly understood, and no others,
that the differing viewpoints within the nation can be
ultimately reconciled.*[96]

Wallace's statements regarding the capstone being 'fitted
into place' were to have a peculiar epilogue at the turn of the
millennium. The Egyptian government announced in 1999 that
the coming New Years Eve would be celebrated by a gala event
at the pyramids at Giza. During a musical performance by Jean-
Michael Jarre – with a theme revolving around the astrological
zodiac – the 'Eye of Horus' was to be projected upon the
pyramids. Then, at midnight, the event would culminate with
a helicopter placing a gold capstone on the Great Pyramid, to
symbolically complete it.

The explicitly Masonic theme of this planned event is
astounding, considering that Freemasonry is outlawed in Egypt.
Sure enough, rumors began that this was a staged event by Masons
to announce the beginning of a New World Order, which former
President George H. W. Bush had alluded to during his term in
office. Once the Egyptian press got hold of the story, the event
was promptly cancelled.

SKULL AND BONES

One of the rumors which coincided with the capstone controversy was that former President George H. W. Bush had planned to be at the Giza complex for the millennium celebrations. Bush had already been singled out by conspiracy theorists for his own 'New World Order' speech, but another piece of information was equally tantalizing. The former President is also a member of the Yale University society 'Skull and Bones', a secret organization with distinctly Masonic overtones.

Skull and Bones was founded in 1832, notable as a time when the Craft was in decline due to the anti-Masonry surrounding the disappearance of William Morgan in 1826. Senior members choose only 15 students each year to become members. Once you are 'tapped', you become a member for life.

The skull and bones imagery appears to have originally come from the Templars. A folk tale dated to the 12th Century outlines the mythical origins of the motif:

> *A great lady of Maraclea was loved by a Templar, a Lord of Sidon; but she died in her youth, and on the night of her burial, this wicked lover crept to the grave, dug up her body and violated it. Then a voice from the void bade him return in nine months time for he would find a son. He obeyed the injunction and at the appointed time he opened the grave again and found a head on the leg bones of the skeleton [the skull and crossbones]. The same voice bade him 'guard it well, for it would be the giver of all good things'…in due course, it passed into the possession of the Order.*[97]

This imagery has since become closely related to Freemasonry. Additionally, the 'Skull and Bones' fraternity at Yale shares a common motto with the Craft: *Memento Mori* (a Latin phrase meaning "remember you must die"). The amazing thing about the 'Skull and Bones' society though, is the immense power held by members, despite the size of the fraternity. If you like to play the numbers game, try this one: there are almost 300 million people living in the United States. And yet the two mainstream Presidential candidates who contested the 2004 election, John Kerry and George W. Bush, are both members of the same secret society which has only 800 or so living members: Skull and Bones.

Respected journalist Tim Russert asked each candidate about their Skull and Bones affiliation on his show 'Meet the Press', prior to the election. George W. Bush answered:

> *It's so secret, we can't talk about it.*[98]

When Russert asked John Kerry what the significance was of both he and Bush being members of the same secret society, Kerry replied:

> *Not much, because it's a secret.*[99]

In light of this 'dual candidacy', it is interesting to note that Antony C. Sutton introduced his seminal book *America's Secret Establishment: An Introduction to the Order of the Skull and Bones* by outlining the organization's basic philosophy for achieving absolute power:

> *If you can control the opposites, you dominate the nature of the outcome.*

Beyond Bush and Kerry though (and not to mention former President George H. W. Bush), there are just as many 'Bonesmen' with powerful connections in the finance sector, intelligence agencies, and the halls of justice. Alexandra Robbins, author of *Secrets of the Tomb*, says that this is the primary goal of the organization: to get as many members as possible into positions of power.

For example, President George W. Bush employed five fellow Bonesmen in his first administration. One of those was William Donaldson, the head of the Securities and Exchange Commission. Society members at one time provided more than a third of the partners in financial heavyweights Morgan Stanley and Brown Brothers Harriman. At least one dozen Bonesmen can be linked to the Federal Reserve, and members also control the wealth of the Rockefeller, Carnegie, and Ford families. Other Bonesmen of note have been the 27th President of the United States, William Howard Taft, and Henry Luce, the founder of Time Magazine.[100]

The influence of Skull and Bones in the intelligence community and foreign affairs is especially impressive – some even claim that Bonesmen were responsible for creating the intelligence 'business' in the United States. The list of Bonesmen who have ties with the Central Intelligence Agency (C.I.A.) is formidable, and includes former President George H. W. Bush, who served as Director of the agency for a period. Considering the inclusion of C.I.A headquarters in the Da Vinci Challenge – via the enigmatic 'Kryptos' sculpture – this may be significant.

In a phone call which sounds like it is straight out of a Dan Brown book, investigative journalist Ron Rosenbaum was warned against prying into the secrets of the Skull and Bones:

> *They don't like people tampering and prying. The power of Bones is incredible. They've got their hands on every lever of power in the country...it's like trying to look into the Mafia.*[101]

Lastly, there is a slight echo here of Brown's *Angels and Demons*, as rumors abound that Bonesmen are branded with a skull and bones motif as part of their initiation. Readers will remember that in *Angels and Demons*, the killer brands Leonardo Vettra with an Illuminati ambigram.

THE DEAD PRESIDENTS

As we have seen, the relatively small society of Skull and Bones has amassed a large degree of power, and has 'contributed' three presidents. Freemasonry, which has a much larger membership, has provided even more influence in the White House. In fact, at least sixteen presidents have been confirmed as Freemasons (excluding the three Skull and Bones members)[102]:

- George Washington, 1st President of the United States
- James Monroe, 5th President of the United States
- Andrew Jackson, 7th President of the United States
- James Knox Polk, 11th President of the United States
- David Rice Atchison, (ex-officio President for one day)
- James Buchanan, 15th President of the United States
- Andrew Johnson, 17th President of the United States
- James Garfield, 20th President of the United States
- William McKinley, 25th President of the United States
- Theodore Roosevelt, 26th President of the United States
- William Howard Taft, 27th President of the United States
- Warren Harding, 29th President of the United States
- Franklin D Roosevelt, 32nd President of the United States
- Harry S Truman, 33rd President of the United States
- Lyndon B Johnson, 36th President of the United States
- Gerald Ford, 40th President of the United States.

Washington on the Dollar Bill

This number does not include less official relationships, such as former President Bill Clinton's involvement in the Masonic youth organization, the Order of DeMolay, or the honorary Scottish Rite membership conferred upon former President Ronald Reagan.

Finally, returning to the Great Seal imagery on the dollar bill, there is one last detail worth noting about the portrayal of President George Washington on the reverse side. David Ovason points out that if you fold the dollar bill vertically, or draw straight diagonals between the tops of the '1' figures, you will find the same point of convergence: directly in the middle of George Washington's right eye. Considering the Da Vinci Challenge on the Internet ended with the explicit request that the contestant click on the Mona Lisa's right eye ('oeil droit'), this detail may well be something Dan Brown has incorporated into *The Solomon Key*.

CHAPTER 7

THE SOLOMON CODES

As we have already noted, a large part of the success of Dan Brown's novels is likely due to the inclusion of puzzles, cryptograms and codes within his novels. As a fan of cryptography, Brown would have a solid grounding in the history of this secret craft, which would no doubt be of assistance when writing his thrillers. For instance, when writing about Leonardo Da Vinci, he employed a puzzle based on the famous painter's penchant for mirror writing.

If we are correct in our predictions for the subject matter of *The Solomon Key,* we can be sure that there will be more of the same, as many of the major 'players' were known to have used or invented codes and ciphers. So too with secretive organizations like Freemasonry, the Essenes and the Knights Templar. Not to mention we know for a fact that Brown included the Kryptos sculpture at C.I.A. headquarters in Langley, Virginia as part of his Internet challenge.

While Sanborn has created ciphers that have remained uncracked for over a decade, we should expect codes that are a little simpler in *The Solomon Key.* As the history of cryptography is mostly one of ever-increasing complexity, we'll start with the earliest candidates for inclusion into Dan Brown's next book, and work our way forward. Let's rewind some two thousand years shall we?

THE ESSENES AND ATBASH

As our investigation into the content of the book has turned up the 'Essenes' as a possibility, it is worth reviewing their link with cryptography. As we discussed earlier, Dr Hugh Schonfield first proposed the decryption of the Templar 'Baphomet' using the Atbash Cipher employed by the Essene sect. This cipher is a straight substitution between two Hebrew alphabets, one written forward and the other in reverse. For example, Bible scholars found that applying the Atbash to the mysterious location of 'Scheschach' resulted in the more recognizable 'Babel'.

This technique is referred to as a 'mono-alphabetic substitution cipher', and similar ciphers were successfully used right up until the Renaissance. Julius Caesar used a related technique for some of his own coded messages (not using Hebrew of course), hence these ciphers are often called 'Caesar shifts'. Though not very complex, and easily cracked by an expert, Caesar shifts proficiently hide messages from 'uneducated' people.

Whether Dan Brown uses the Atbash Cipher is another question – he has already explained it in *The Da Vinci Code*, so perhaps expect something new in its place.

FRANCIS BACON

We have already seen that Sir Francis Bacon was a politician, a scientist, and a philosopher who held the Utopian goal which seems to run through our investigation. But Bacon was also deeply interested in cryptography, and used a number of cipher methods and personal codes in his writings. Perhaps not just 'his' writings either – a number of researchers attribute the works of Shakespeare to him, on the basis of numerous similarities.

The esoteric expert Manly P. Hall devotes a number of chapters to Bacon in his masterpiece, *The Secret Teachings of All Ages*. One chapter deals with the Bacon-Shakespeare theory, while another delves into his cryptographic methods. We will draw much of our information from this book, as it is written in reference to Bacon's Rosicrucian leanings. Incidentally, Dan Brown is definitely familiar with Baconian ciphers, as in *The Da Vinci Code* he writes that:

> Langdon had once worked on a series of Baconian manuscripts that contained epigraphical ciphers in which certain lines of code were clues as to how to decipher the other lines.[103]

In *The Secret Teachings of All Ages,* Manly Hall outlines a number of different cipher systems employed by Francis Bacon:

Biliteral Ciphers:

Bacon's most famous contribution to cryptography is his 'biliteral cipher', first described in *De Augmentis Scientiarum* in 1605. Bacon thought that obvious ciphers, where the passage was an unreadable mess of letters, only encouraged people to investigate further. Instead he thought that ciphers should "be without suspicion" – that is, the person reading the encoded message should not be aware a cipher is present, unless properly trained to do so. This technique is often referred to as steganography.

Bacon's biliteral cipher is based around the use of just two letters, 'a' and 'b', which are used in five-character combinations to designate each letter of the alphabet. For example, the letter 'f' might be ciphered as 'aabba' in the biliteral system. Bacon's cipher is an early example of the binary code which now rules our world, via computers, and is also a precursor to the dots and dashes of Morse code.

Bacon's biliteral cipher combined this idea of binary coding with a process of font encoding, whereby two different font types would be used when publishing a manuscript. One font was the 'a' font, the other the 'b', and as such the five-letter biliteral 'words' could be encoded into any text to be printed – no matter what its literary content – by simply manipulating the fonts. To explain it simplistically, let's use a lower case font as our 'a', and upper case as the 'b' font. This will of course make the cipher blatantly obvious – proper use entails keeping upper and lower case as normal and employing only subtle differences between the fonts.

In our example, we will use five arbitrary letter combinations to designate the letters C,D,E,O and S:

C = aaaba
D = aaabb
E = aabaa
O = abbab
S = baaab

Using the passage 'Francis Bacon was Shakespeare', our encoded message would be published like this:

FRAnCIs bAcON Was SHaKEsPEAre

Here's the explanation of how the cipher works: separating the sentence into five letter groups (with one left over which we will ignore), we can see the parallel between the font encoding and the biliteral cipher words:

FRAnC IsbAc ONWas SHaKE sPEAre
aaaba   abbab   aaabb   aabaa   baaab
C   O   D   E   S

Our encoded word is therefore – CODES. As mentioned above, our example is intentionally obvious. If you would like to test your powers of observation, a more realistic example of using two different fonts might look like this:

Francis Bacon was Shakespeare

In *De Augmentis Scientiarum*, Bacon actually used an example where even the encoded word was replaced by a simple substitution cipher, just to further complicate the decoding sequence and thereby discourage crackers.[104]

The Alchemical Cipher:

In reality, the alchemical cipher is simply a literal cipher – that is, one to do with the arrangement or combination of letters of the alphabet.[105] Manly Hall gives a couple of examples of this sort of cryptogram, both of which are composed of circular diagrams combined with words. By reading the first letter of each word, a hidden code is revealed.

For example, an alchemical cryptogram composed by the Jesuit scholar Athanasius Kircher shows a number of Latin words running around its circular perimeter: *Sola, Vera, Laudat, Philosophia, Homines, Veritatis, Rectae.* If the reader picks out the first letter of each word they will find the word SVLPHVR – 'sulphur', once the 'V' is transposed to a 'u'. Continuing with the rest of the words on the diagram, the final decoded combination of words is *Sulphur Fixum Est Sol*, or 'Fixed Sulphur is Gold' – a definite alchemical phrase, and as such worthy of hiding from 'profane eyes'. This technique is similar to the 'acrostic', whereby the first letter of each line in a manuscript is read to reveal the hidden message.

We can see a relationship here with the anagram of MASON found on the Great Seal (see page 97). The geometric overlay of the Seal of Solomon on the Great Seal reveals the anagram from the curved text, 'for those with eyes to see': MASON.

Pictorial Ciphers:

Manly Hall describes pictorial ciphers as "any picture or drawing with other than its obvious meaning", and categorizes the diagrams of alchemists as such.[106] They can take many forms – the number of bricks in a wall, the fold of a person's clothes,

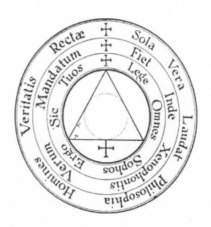

Alchemical Cipher of Athanasius Kircher

the position of the subject's fingers, and structures in the form of letters (such as the alleged "M" found within *The Last Supper*).

One such enciphered code was the initials 'AA', which can be seen in a number of Rosicrucian diagrams and headpieces, including some works of Shakespeare, and which has particular meaning for those in the Rosicrucian tradition. It can also be found in some of Bacon's philosophical works. Another favourite of Bacon's was, fittingly enough, the image of a hog.

Numerical Ciphers:

The simplest numerical cipher is one in which the letters of the alphabet are substituted with their corresponding numbers: A=1, B=2, C=3 etc. In the Baconian system, both 'I' and 'J' are both equivalent to 9, and 'U' and 'V' are both 20. In our case, the keyword CODES would thus become 3-14-4-5-18. The keyword could be further obscured by inserting a pre-arranged number of non-significant characters – for example, inserting one 'fake' number between each real one: 3-2-14-20-4-8-5-10-18.

Important words in this system would then also become recognizable by a single number: the sum of their components. For example, using our keyword CODES, we have 3+14+4+5+18 = 44. This is of course using the simplest version of the numerical cipher – tables of correspondence between letters and arbitrary number values can be developed for a more complex cipher.

Manly Hall points out that authors of numerical cryptograms can also create a 'signature number' from the numerical value of their own names.[107] For example, Francis Bacon is said to have regularly used the number 33 – the numerical equivalent of 'Bacon'. The author of a coded message can therefore 'sign' his work by an in-joke, such as some glaring error on that particular page number, word number or combination of both.

Bacon also employed the number 287 as a personal motif. In his *Advancement of Learning*, there are 287 letters on the frontispiece, 287 letters on the Dedication page, and 287 letters on the page numbered 215 – which is actually falsely numbered and is really page 287.[108]

KABBALAH AND MAGICK

Both Rosicrucians and Freemasons are known to have been influenced by the system of Jewish mysticism called the Kabbalah. The numerical cipher mentioned above has its roots in the Kabbalistic technique of Gematria. Hebrew mystics saw great truths in the numerical equivalent of words, even to the point where the sum of two words which equaled another would constitute a definite relationship. For example, the Hebrew words *aheva* ('love') and *echod* ('one') are both numerically equivalent in Gematria to the number 13. The name of God, *YHVH* or *Jehovah*, is equal to 26. Thus, God = one love.[109]

A second technique, the Notarikon, is a system of creating a new word from the components of a group of other words. Many of our modern-day acronyms basically fit into this system (minus the Hebrew language aspect of course). A good example of the Notarikon is a biblical word known to most of us, 'Amen'. Amen is a composite of three words: *Al, Melech* and *Neh-eh-mahn* (A.M.N.) meaning 'God is our faithful king'.[110]

The third Kabbalistic method we should mention is called Temurah. This is basically a straight substitution cipher, with letters transposed into corresponding characters according to a set system.[111] The Atbash cipher is one of a number of methods described by Temurah.

Lastly, we should quickly discuss one final technique of encoding words as graphics, which rather than serving as a cryptogram was in fact used for Talismanic magick. While discussing a system of magick in our investigation may seem a little off-center, we only have to see the title of our main reference work on Talismanic magick to see the relevance: *Clavicula Salomonis*, or 'The Key of Solomon'.

This book was put back together by occult writer S. Liddell Macgregor Mathers in 1888, from manuscripts in the British Museum. In his preface, he states that he has no reason to doubt the attribution of this magical system to King Solomon, noting that the Jewish historian Josephus recognized that Solomon was versed in occult practices. The book begins with these words:

> *Everyone knoweth in the present day that from time immemorial Solomon possessed knowledge inspired by the wise teachings of an angel...near his end, he left to his son Roboam a Testament which should contain all (the Wisdom) he had possessed prior to his death. The Rabbins, who were careful to cultivate (the same knowledge) after him, called this Testament the Clavicle or Key of Solomon, which they caused to be engraved on (pieces of) the bark of trees, while the Pentacles were inscribed in Hebrew letters on plates of copper, so that they might be carefully preserved in the Temple which that wise king had caused to be built.*[112]

The Key of Solomon describes these pentacles with sigils – that is, line drawings – as being constructed by tracing the letters of a name, via numerical correspondence, over a magic square (a square in which each row or column of numbers adds to the same amount).

Whole books have been written about the construction of talismans and sigils, however we will only mention it here in passing as a topic that could be covered by Dan Brown in *The Solomon Key*.

THE MASONIC CIPHER

Manly Hall mentions in *The Secret Teachings of All Ages* that Freemasons were known to have used a number of secret alphabets, including 'Angelic' and 'Celestial' writing. However, one secret alphabet in particular was used so much by the Craft that it came to be known as the Masonic Cipher. Also called the Pigpen Cipher, this technique was used widely by 18th Century Masons, for keeping private correspondence secret. The Masonic Cipher substitutes each letter for a symbol, with the symbol being a description of where the letter is placed on the 'pigpen grid'. Two letters are placed in each grid space, with the second letter being designated by both the shape of the grid space as well as a dot.

Note that there are many different ways of laying out the letters on the pigpen grid, so each will encode differently. The two most common are the 'English method', whereby the letters are placed in the grid squares two at a time ('ab', 'cd' etc.), and the 'American method', which runs through the alphabet one 'square' at a time (thus typical grid squares are 'an', 'bo' etc).

Dan Brown is also familiar with the Masonic cipher, as it was used in a challenge on his website.[113]

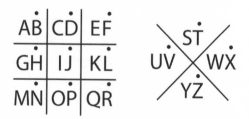

'English' Masonic Cipher Example

The Jefferson Wheel Cipher

Jefferson, like Benjamin Franklin, was a keen inventor. While serving as the United States Secretary of State under the Presidency of George Washington, Jefferson created his own cipher method. As mail at the time was very insecure, secrecy was paramount when communicating affairs of the nation. Jefferson's idea was the encryption of a message using a 'wheel cipher'.

Jefferson's invention consisted of a number of flat wooden disks, each around ½ inch in thickness, layered together using an iron spindle through their center (to visualize this, imagine a spindle of blank CDs on its side...only the CDs are much thicker than normal). The complete alphabet was inscribed on the edge of each disk in random order. By spelling out the cipher message across one row by turning each disk into place, twenty-five separate encoded phrases were therefore available to be chosen from the other rows on the disk. [114]

Someone with the same arrangement of disks and letters would then be able to spell out the encoded phrase on their cipher wheel, and then scan the other rows for one that made sense.

Beyond the 'Jefferson Wheel Cipher', the third President of the United States also used the well-known Vigenère method of encoding messages. If Dan Brown's next book is truly about the Founding Fathers, then there is certainly a good chance that Jefferson's use of codes will be mentioned.

James Sanborn

In *Angels and Demons*, Dan Brown employed graphic designer John Langdon to create distinct motifs, called 'ambigrams', for his book. Langdon's ambigrams are words that are designed so that the same word can be read when it is upside-down. In the acknowledgements for the book, Brown thanks him for rising "to my impossible challenge" – and gave further credit by giving his lead character the artist's surname.

It may be that Brown is working in a similar manner with artist James Sanborn for *The Solomon Key*. As we discussed at the beginning of the book, Sanborn is the creator of the enigmatic 'Kryptos' sculpture which sits at C.I.A. headquarters in Langley, Virginia. Not only is Kryptos mentioned in the Da Vinci Challenge, but rumors on the Internet have said that Brown is working closely with Sanborn on *The Solomon Key*.

Firstly, considering the location of the Kryptos sculpture and the fact that Sanborn works out of Washington, D.C., Brown may be planning on actually using one of Sanborn's cryptographic sculptures in the setting of his book. It could even be the case that Brown has commissioned a new sculpture from him expressly for *The Solomon Key*, which would provide great publicity – a case of fiction becoming reality.

Secondly, if Brown does use the Kryptos sculpture in the book, he may be expected to draw on the mysterious messages so far decoded from it for parts of his plot. For example, the third deciphered passage reads:

> *Slowly, desperately slowly, the remains of passage debris that encumbered the lower part of the doorway was removed. With trembling hands I made a tiny breach in the upper left-hand corner. And then, widening the hole a little, I inserted the candle and peered in. The hot air escaping from the chamber caused the flame to flicker, but presently details of the room within emerged from the mist. Can you see anything?*[115]

This message appears to be a paraphrase of the diary entry of Howard Carter on November 26th 1922 – the day he discovered the tomb of the Pharaoh Tutankhamen ('King Tut') at Luxor in Egypt.[116] The reference to secret chambers, and the tie-in to Egypt, is the sort of subject matter that would work well in *The Solomon Key*.

Lastly, if James Sanborn is involved with Dan Brown's next novel, we should at least expect that any codes he produces will be a little easier than the Kryptos sculpture. The last enciphered message on Kryptos has remained uncracked for thirteen years...

THE REST

Again, it should be noted that we are attempting to predict the subjects that Dan Brown might use – however, as a fiction writer he can draw from any source he wants, or even invent one. Naturally, we cannot explore every possible cryptography device which Brown might be likely to use. But we can at least run through a number of related topics that might also make an appearance in the novel.

For a start, Brown certainly has some favourite ciphers, at least for presenting puzzles to the public. As devices for his novel and website challenges, these are generally quite simple. For example, he has used the 'Caesar Box' technique, and also relies on anagrams quite a bit. We might therefore expect other similar techniques to be used in *The Solomon Key*.

If we are right with our topic predictions, there are also a number of numerical ciphers which stand out. Both Francis Bacon and Freemasonry are said to have employed the number 33 as a 'signature', while Skull and Bones members apparently use the number 322 as their own personal motif.

However, many other numbers are also significant. For instance, 13 plays an important role in the symbolism of the Great Seal and in Freemasonry, and is also the date of

Philippe's attack on the Templars. Also, 32 is a number linking Scottish Rite Freemasonry with both the Kabbalah and Tarot. In *Talisman,* Hancock and Bauval cite the 33rd degree Scottish Rite author Charles Sumner Lobingier – the historian for the Grand Commandery in Washington, D.C. – as saying that in the 32 'paths of wisdom' in the Kabbalah "we doubtless have the origin of the number of degrees as formulated by the Grand Constitution of the Scottish Rite."[117]

If the subject matter includes the Rosicrucians, then this number symbolism could also be applied to curious riddles ready-made for a Dan Brown thriller. In the Rosicrucian document *The Chymical Wedding* there are a number of alphabetical riddles based on numerical ciphers. For example:

> *My name contains five and fifty, and yet hath only eight letters.*

The 17th Century scientist Leibnitz is said to have solved this riddle using the Kabbalistic method of Gematria, proposing the answer ALCHIMIA (alchemy).[118] If the Rosicrucians play a part in *The Solomon Key*, such linguistic riddles may be a handy plot device for Brown.

If Skull and Bones are used in the novel then we may also see the use of classical names to identify the protagonists. This aspect of the Skull and Bones society is similar to the use of coded names by the Bavarian Illuminati: Adam Weishaupt went under the pseudonym of Spartacus, Baron von Knigge was Philo, their headquarters was called Eleusis. Dan Brown hinted that he knew this piece of history in *Angels and Demons*, as the arch-villain of the novel used the pseudonym Janus when contacting his hired killer, the Hassassin. Incidentally, this was an apt name for the villain, as Janus was a Roman god with two faces.

After the dissolution of the Knights Templar, some claim that the organization was regrouped by Jean-Marc Larmenius. A document, known as the Larmenius Charter, appears to show a list of Templar Grand Masters subsequent to the death of Jacques de Molay. This charter was written in ciphered Latin, with a secret alphabet employed as the encoding device.[119] Considering its providence, it might be seen as worthy of inclusion by Brown – although the Masonic Cipher is probably far more likely.

If the Illuminati reappear in this Robert Langdon story, then another cipher script which may be used is the 'Illuminati Cipher' as described in *A History of Secret Societies,* written by Akron Daraul (a pseudonym of Idries Shah). This cipher has gained some prominence through the work of Robert Anton Wilson, who embedded it within some of the illustrations in his best-selling book *Cosmic Trigger.*[120]

Finally, it is natural that the puzzles created by Dan Brown for *The Solomon Key* could well rely on Egyptian, Rosicrucian and Masonic symbolism. The main character, Robert Langdon, is after all a 'symbologist'. To run through the vast iconography of these traditions is beyond the scope of this book, however the obvious motifs are:

- Seal of Solomon
- Masonic Square and Compass
- Twin Pillars of Boaz and Jachin
- Skull and Crossbones
- Pyramid
- All-seeing eye
- Pentagram
- Rosy-Cross

It will be interesting to see how close we have got!

CHAPTER 8

OTHER TOPICS

In the course of our investigation, we have predicted the topics of *The Solomon Key* based mainly upon Dan Brown's own statements and hints given in the website challenge. However, once we consider these main subjects – Freemasonry, the Founding Fathers, Kryptos – a number of related topics present themselves. While it is difficult to predict whether Dan Brown will include these 'second-tier' topics in *The Solomon Key*, it is probably worth mentioning some of them here briefly, as at least being worthy of inclusion in the coming novel. So to finish off, let's take a quick look at some of these subjects.

THE JESUITS

We have discussed many aspects of the possible content of *The Solomon Key*, but one item we have not yet covered is the possible villain. In *The Da Vinci Code*, this role was played by the albino Silas, an Opus Dei operative. While the arch-villain of the novel simply used Opus Dei to fulfill his objectives, Dan

Brown still used the negative aspects of the order – for instance, corporeal mortification – to good effect in creating the 'dark side' of the Catholic Church.

If Brown is to follow the same formula in the sequel to *The Da Vinci Code*, then he may be tempted to use the Society of Jesus – better known as the Jesuits – as the villain. For despite this Christian society's fine reputation for charitable missionary work and contributions to education, some researchers have also alleged that there is a seedy underbelly to the order. Some of the aspects of this alleged 'dark side' would certainly suit a Dan Brown thriller, especially when we consider that the Jesuits are also said to have been in a running battle against Freemasonry throughout their history.

The Society of Jesus is a Catholic organization which was formed in 1534 by a University of Paris graduate student named Ignatius of Loyola, in response to the spread of the Protestant Reformation. Loyola and his small group bound themselves to a vow of chastity and poverty, and dedicated their work to the Catholic mission. They received papal approval in 1537, permitting them to be ordained as priests.

The Jesuit *Constitutions* is the official guide for members of the society. This document creates an organization of priests completely devoted in obedience to the Pope and the Catholic Church. Some 'alternative history' researchers have said that in this devotion we find the darker side of the Society of Jesus, as some of the oaths allegedly taken by Jesuit priests encourage an 'anything goes' approach to defending Catholicism. In a ceremony known as the 'Extreme Oath' (of which it must be said there is little substantial evidence), the presiding superior allegedly says these words to the initiate:

My son, heretofore you have been taught to act the dissembler: among Roman Catholics to be a Roman

Catholic, and to be a spy even among your own brethren;
to believe no man, to trust no man. Among the Reformers,
to be a reformer…among the Calvinists, to be a Calvinist;
among other Protestants, generally to be a Protestant, and
obtaining their confidence, to seek even to preach from their
pulpits, and to denounce with all the vehemence in your
nature our Holy Religion and the Pope; and even to descend
so low as to become a Jew among Jews, that you might be
enabled to gather together all information for the benefit of
your Order as a faithful soldier of the Pope.[121]

This supposed mission of the Jesuits to infiltrate other religious groups and cultures has led to accusations that they did so with Freemasonry and the Illuminati in the 18th Century (interestingly, Adam Weishaupt was a former Jesuit). Despite the tenuous evidence for such claims, this does provide a viable link between Dan Brown's latest subject matter and the Jesuits. It would also allow Brown the plot device of insinuating that a certain group, in this case Freemasonry, is guilty of crimes, when in fact it was a Jesuit infiltrator inciting chaos. The alleged Extreme Oath continues:

You have been taught to insidiously plant the seeds of jealousy
and hatred between communities, provinces, states that were
at peace, and incite them to deeds of blood, involving them
in war with each other, and to create revolutions and civil
wars in countries that were independent and prosperous.[122]

Considering Brown's penchant for religious assassins (featuring in both Robert Langdon books – one Islamic, the other from Opus Dei), one particular section of the alleged Extreme Oath gives him ample opportunity to create another in the same mold:

I will have no opinion or will of my own, or any mental reservation whatever, even as a corpse or cadaver, but will unhesitatingly obey each and every command that I may receive from my superiors in the Militia of the Pope and of Jesus Christ...I furthermore promise and declare that I will, when opportunity present, make and wage relentless war, secretly or openly, against all heretics...I will hang, waste, boil, flay, strangle and bury alive these infamous heretics, rip up the stomachs and wombs of their women and crush their infants' heads against the walls, in order to annihilate forever their execrable race.[123]

Whether the Extreme Oath is a genuine part of the modern Society of Jesus, or if Jesuits have really engaged in such practices in the United States, is not of any consequence to Brown. As we have seen, his previous books are built on the accusations and assumptions found throughout 'alternative history' research, and as he writes fiction he has a degree of poetic license to improvise on these themes – whether or not they are true. Some writers have also claimed that the Jesuits acted as political assassins, so we should repeat here that the plot of *The Solomon Key* is said to revolve around the murder of several current political leaders by someone with ties to the Freemasons.[124]

Speaking of the Founding Fathers, consider this letter from John Adams, the second President of the United States, to Thomas Jefferson, regarding the Society of Jesus which had just been reformed by the Pope:

Their restoration is indeed a step toward darkness, cruelty, perfidy, despotism, death...I do not like the reappearance of the Jesuits...Shall we not have regular swarms of them here, in as many disguises as only a king of the gypsies can assume, dressed as printers, publishers, writers and schoolmasters? If ever there was a body of men who merited damnation on earth and in Hell, it is this society of Loyola's. Nevertheless, we are compelled by our system of religious toleration to offer them an asylum.[125]

Two relevant points before finishing: firstly, one of the great scientific and cryptographic minds of the 17ᵗʰ Century was the Jesuit priest Athanasius Kircher. Secondly, Georgetown University in Washington, D.C. is a Jesuit institution.

Oak Island

Oak Island lies in Mahone Bay in Nova Scotia, Canada. It is famed for supposedly concealing a treasure which remains undiscovered after two centuries of exploration. The story goes that in 1795 a teenager discovered a circular depression on the island with a tree above it, which had a pulley system hanging from a branch. The teenager dug into the depression with some friends, and discovered a layer of flagstones, and then a layer of logs about every ten feet after that. At thirty feet they abandoned the dig, but returned eight years later after forming a company with the express intention of recovering whatever lay beneath. They continued on until the dig was ninety feet in depth, finding charcoal, clay and coconut husk fibers at 40, 50 and 60 feet respectively.

At this depth a bizarre find was made – a stone covered in some sort of unknown symbols. The pit also suddenly flooded with water back up to around the thirty feet mark. The flooding was found to have been caused by a 500-foot-long tunnel leading from the pit to a nearby cove.

From this point the tale becomes repetitive, with numerous companies trying to recover the buried 'treasure' only to be repelled by the water flooding back into the pit. Six people have lost their lives excavating on Oak Island. One of the few successes was made by the 'Triton Alliance', which in 1976 excavated a 237-foot deep shaft, lowering down a camera to view the excavation. They allegedly viewed some chests, some tools and a human hand. However, the shaft collapsed and the project was subsequently abandoned. [126]

What is the 'treasure' of Oak Island? There are many theories, but one in particular is relevant to the topics in Dan Brown's *The Solomon Key*. Some say that the treasure is that of the Knights Templar, removed from France prior to King Philippe's attack, and brought to the Americas on the missing boats of the Templar fleet. Remember though, that this would have the Templars sailing to America more than 150 years before Columbus.

There is also a connection with Rosslyn Chapel: there is a story, called the Zeno Narrative, that Henry Sinclair – the grandfather of the founder of Rosslyn Chapel William St Clair – sailed to Nova Scotia with an Italian navigator by the name of Antonio Zeno. This voyage was said to have taken place in 1398, almost a century before Columbus. Supporters of this theory cite the carvings in Rosslyn Chapel of maize, a New World plant species which was unknown in Britain at the time, as well as the so-called 'Westford Knight' engraving in Massachusetts – which is said to depict a Templar Knight.

If either the Templars or Sinclair made this journey, what was the reason? Some say it was simply to move the treasure of the Paris Templars. Others say it was to move the 'Holy Grail', or religious documents found by the Knights Templar in Jerusalem. And there is also a theory that these were 'scouting missions', attempting to find a new land where the Templar Utopia could be built.

On the flip-side, the well-known skeptic Joe Nickell has pointed out that Oak Island is largely a Masonic affair. In an article for *Skeptical Inquirer,* Nickell pointed out that a number of those attempting to excavate the 'Money Pit' were Masons or had ties to the Craft. Beyond that though, the whole 'myth' of Oak Island has a number of direct parallels to the 'secret vault' story found in Royal Arch Masonry, and also with the nearby treasure mystery of the 'Beale Papers' of Virginia.[127] He suggests that elements of the story have been embellished to reflect the Masonic myth. As a side note, those who have watched the movie *National Treasure* might be interested by the fact that the Beale mystery involves a cipher written on the Declaration of Independence...

One final point worth noting: Franklin Delano Roosevelt, a former President of the United States and 32nd degree Freemason, went treasure hunting on Oak Island in 1909 with the 'Old Gold Salvage' group, and is said to have kept up with developments on the state of excavations for the rest of his life.[128]

However, despite the mass of fascinating material available on Oak Island for Brown to incorporate into *The Solomon Key,* he may be persuaded not to do so due to the release, in late 2004, of the aforementioned movie *National Treasure* starring Nicholas Cage. The movie covers some of the same territory as Brown's next novel, such as the Founding Fathers and the all-seeing eye, as well as the discovery of the fabled Templar treasure in a secret chamber deep underground. Ironically, many people accused *National Treasure* of being a copy of *The Da Vinci Code* when it was first released – however, it was already in production before the book became a hit.

Albert Pike and the Ku Klux Klan

Within the House of the Temple in Washington, D.C. lays the body of Confederate general Albert Pike. The privileged resting place is a testament to Pike's contribution to the Scottish Rite, Southern Jurisdiction – he composed the ritual, and was the presiding Sovereign Grand Commander of the group from 1859 until his death in 1891.

A lawyer and newspaper editor, Pike also authored a number of books on Freemasonry. The best known of these is *Morals and Dogma*, a book which was meant as a supplement to the rituals he designed for the Scottish Rite, Southern Jurisdiction. The content is a rambling commentary on ancient cultures and comparative religion, and the book was given to each initiate after they gained entrance to the 14th degree. It's interesting to note that one section of Pike's treatise is concerned with the similarities between the myths and iconography of the Egyptian goddess Isis, and the subsequent Marian tradition of Christianity.

Morals and Dogma has gained quite a reputation among conspiracy theorists and anti-Masons, due largely to the fraudulent writings of a Frenchman calling himself Léo Taxil (real name Gabriel Pagès). After originally writing a number of anti-Catholic tracts, Taxil subsequently turned his attention to Freemasonry, and focused particularly on Albert Pike. He fraudulently attributed to Pike the worship of Lucifer, and designated him as the 'Sovereign Pontiff of Universal Freemasonry'. Taxil claimed the existence of an ultra-secret sect of Masons named Palladium. However, in 1897 he revealed that his writings were hoaxes. Perhaps tellingly, Taxil was schooled by the Jesuits.

Nevertheless, there are many sections of *Morals and Dogma* which show that Pike was very interested in the occult, and his writings on the 'Luciferian philosophy' have no doubt provided plenty of fuel for anti-Masons. However, it is important to note that Pike's reverence for the Lucifer principle was not referring to the the Christian idea of the devil, but instead to the classical definition of a search for light, or knowledge. The ancient

Romans named the morning star, Venus, as Lucifer: literally, 'the shining one'.

Pike also appeared to believe in a 'hierarchy of knowing', and wrote with disdain on much of Blue Masonry (the first three degrees). For instance:

> *The Blue Degrees are but the outer court or portico of the Temple. Part of the symbols are displayed there to the Initiate, but he is intentionally misled by false interpretations...their true explication is reserved for the Adepts, the Princes of Masonry...Masonry is the veritable Sphinx, buried to the head in the sands heaped round it by the ages.*

Pike's writings show that he was deeply interested in the Kabbalah and other strands of Hermetic thinking. As we noted earlier, the historian of the Scottish Rite, Southern Jurisdiction sees the 32 degrees of the order's ritual as being based upon the '32 paths of wisdom' in the Kabbalah. Pike also sided with the anti-Catholic thinking of many of the medieval occultists and scientists:

> *Masonry is a search after Light. That search leads us directly back, as you see, to the Kabbalah. In that ancient and little understood medley of absurdity and philosophy, the Initiate will find the source of doctrines; and may in time come to understand the Hermetic philosophers, the Alchemist, all the Anti-Papal thinkers of the Middle Ages...*

Beyond these controversial philosophies however, Albert Pike is also embroiled in another, far stranger debate. In 1993, a group petitioned the Council of the District of Columbia to remove a statue of Albert Pike that sits in Judiciary Square in Washington, D.C. Their request was made on the basis that Albert Pike was one of the founders of the infamous Ku Klux Klan.

The Ku Klux Klan organization that we recognize today, replete with burning crosses, white hoods and lynch mobs, is actually the third incarnation of a group originally founded in Tennessee in 1865, after the end of the American Civil War. Confederate veterans originally created the group to achieve a number of goals: to aid Confederate widows and orphans of the war, to oppose the extension of voting rights to Blacks, and also to fight other 'impositions' on the southern states during the Reconstruction.

However, the group became known for its use of violence to achieve some of its goals, and in 1871 President Ulysses S. Grant signed The Klan Act, which authorized the use of force to end the terrorist actions of the Klan. This legislation heralded the end of the original Klan, although it was to rise again from the discontent brewing at the start of the 20th Century.

Ku Klux Klan March, Pennsylvania Avenue 1928

The second incarnation of the KKK arrived during World War I, and was a far more successful affair. Many whites living in poverty were drawn to the group through the propaganda that their living conditions were caused by Blacks, Jews, Catholics and foreigners. The group claimed influence in the highest circles of government, allegedly inducting former President Warren Harding, and also almost wooing former President (and 33rd Degree Mason) Harry Truman. At its peak, the KKK boasted some four million members.

The most recent group going under the name of the Ku Klux Klan was not founded until after World War II, and is in essence an organization formed in response to the fledgling civil rights movement of that time. Though it shares commonalities with the original KKK, such as the desire for segregation of races, it is in reality a very separate group. Any attempt to discredit Pike on the basis of his alleged role in the original KKK therefore is not really worthy of consideration, as we must consider that Pike's thinking was shared by most people in the southern states at that time (although that certainly does not validate their philosophy!). It's also worth noting that Pike was an early supporter of the rights of Native Americans.

But was Pike even involved with the original Ku Klux Klan? The only evidence linking him with the group are the writings of a number of pro-Confederate historians from the turn of the century. There is no direct evidence that he founded the group, and it must be remembered that these historians tended to glorify the Confederate role, including the Ku Klux Klan.

Nevertheless, there is some strange history linking Albert Pike with the first incarnation of the KKK. When the anti-Catholic 'Know-Nothings' group – responsible for the theft of the 'Pope Stone' in the Washington monument – dissolved, one of its members formed a new organization. The 'Knights of the Golden Circle' was formed by a 'Know-Nothing' from Virginia named George Bickley in 1856, although others have claimed that Albert Pike himself formed the group. Its aim was American (or more correctly, Southern) expansionism: a circle on the globe some 16 degrees in radius, and centered on Havana in Cuba, was earmarked as territory that should become part of America. This circle included Mexico, Central America and even some of South America. It is alleged that the infamous outlaw Jesse James was a member of the Knights of the Golden Circle.[129]

A curious aspect of Bickley's plan was his use of the number 32. He set up 32 local chapters of his new group, and the 'golden circle' itself was 32 degrees in diameter. The KGC army was also to be composed of two divisions of 16,000 soldiers each – 32,000 altogether. Is there a link here to General Pike? As we have already noted, the 32 normal degrees of Scottish Rite Masonry, devised by Albert Pike, are said to have their basis in the 32 paths of wisdom in the Kabbalah.

In their book *Shadow of the Sentinel*, Bob Brewer and Warren Getler describe how the Knights of the Golden Circle amassed a fortune through various means, and how they hid this treasure in secret caches when the group had to go underground. The knowledge of the whereabouts of the treasure was hidden in a series of complex ciphers, waiting to be reclaimed by initiates when the time was right. Certainly prime fodder for a Dan Brown plot, although whether he is familiar with this obscure piece of history is not known.

It is alleged that the Knights of the Golden Circle eventually morphed into the original Ku Klux Klan. There is circumstantial evidence to support this: they shared many of the same goals, were both based on Confederate idealism, and 'Ku Klux' is actually derived from the Greek work *kyklos*, meaning 'circle'. Note too that the Know-Nothings, the Knights of the Golden Circle, Pike's Scottish Rite Masonry and the Ku Klux Klan all shared a dislike of Catholicism. Many Masons were members of the second incarnation of the Ku Klux Klan, a fact which led the leaders of Freemasonry to purposefully distance themselves from an official affiliation.

The distrust of the Catholic Church by Scottish Rite Masons has continued into recent history. In 1960, the Sovereign Grand Commander of the Scottish Rite, Southern Jurisdiction, wrote an article concerning the possible election of John F. Kennedy, a Catholic, as President. The article appeared in the February 1960 issue of *New Age*, a Masonic publication:

> *Whatever bigotry is in evidence in the United States is exhibited solely by the Roman Catholic hierarchy…the dual allegiance of American Catholics is a present danger to our free institutions…among American citizens there should be no question or suspicion of allegiance to any foreign power, but in the case of the Roman Catholic citizen, his church is the guardian of his conscience and asserts that he must obey its laws and decrees even if they are in conflict with the Constitution and laws of the United States.*

The more fervent conspiracy theorists have taken this statement, in combination with the relatively large number of Masons involved in the JFK assassination investigation, to concoct the theory that Freemasonry (or better still, the Illuminati) was responsible for the former President's murder. However, we must remember that the anti-Catholic sentiments we read here were actually shared by the majority of Protestant Americans at the time. Nevertheless, Dan Brown may be tempted to make some reference to these conspiracy theories.

Woodrow Wilson and the Secret Cabal

A further link with the Ku Klux Klan which is worthy of discussion is that former President Woodrow Wilson had a hand in the success of the second incarnation of the group. His administration was the first to institute segregation in the federal government since Abraham Lincoln began desegregation in 1863, requiring photographs from job applicants in order to determine their race. Wilson's praise of the movie *Birth of a Nation,* which romanticized the original Ku Klux Klan and the Confederate cause, was influential in the re-formation of the organization. Wilson wrote of the film:

> *It is like writing history with lightning, and my only regret is that it is all so true.*

There is no real link here to the Knights of the Golden Circle, but there is still the possibility of a tie-in with *The Solomon Key.* Remember that the Kryptos sculpture referenced by the Da Vinci Challenge has this text encoded:

> *It's buried out there somewhere. Who knows the exact location? Only WW knows.*

While most have assumed that WW refers to former C.I.A chief William Webster, we could also tentatively add Woodrow Wilson to our list of possibilities. Especially as there is a secondary link to Brown's material, a quote from Woodrow Wilson which is regularly quoted by conspiracy theorists regarding the Illuminati. In *The New Freedom,* published in 1913, Wilson wrote:

Since I entered politics, I have chiefly had men's views confided to me privately. Some of the biggest men in the United States, in the Field of commerce and manufacture, are afraid of something. They know that there is a power somewhere so organized, so subtle, so watchful, so interlocked, so complete, so pervasive, that they better not speak above their breath when they speak in condemnation of it.[130]

Ironically, many conspiracy theorists also place Wilson as part of the Illuminati conspiracy, due to his involvement in the creation of the 'League of Nations', which would later become the United Nations. Some of the more paranoid conspiracy theorists see in the United Nations the beginnings of the Illuminati's 'One World Government'. It is difficult, however, to reconcile Wilson's conspiracy quote with his alleged involvement with the Illuminati.

In Brown's hints that Freemasonry and Washington, D.C. will be the central theme of *The Solomon Key*, there is little to suggest that this obscure historical trivia will be in the new book. Nevertheless, the involvement of a 'WW' and the Illuminati certainly make it worth mentioning here.

JOSEPH SMITH AND THE MORMONS

As mentioned earlier, the Da Vinci Challenge on Dan Brown's website used as one of its answers the phrase "Is there no help for the widows son?" This appears to be a blatant reference to Freemasonry, as it is a standard 'distress call' used by the brethren to enlist help. However, there is another possible link.

In New York during the Autumn of 1830, a new religion was born, the Church of Christ – later to become known as the Church of Jesus Christ of Latter Day Saints, also referred to as Mormonism. Its founder was Joseph Smith. While the life story of Joseph Smith is worthy of its own book, we are interested here only in his death.

In 1844 Smith was being held for his own protection in Carthage Jail, Illinois. Despite this measure, a mob of around 200 armed men stormed the prison, and rushed to Smith's cell, firing bullets into the door. Smith was shot several times as he attempted to escape from the mob by jumping from the second story window to his cell. It was reported that as he fell from the window, he was heard to cry "is there no help for the widow's son?"[131]

This is actually no surprise – Joseph Smith was a Freemason and he was probably calling for any Masons in the mob to come to his aid. However, it has become quite a well-known story, and deserves retelling seeing as the phrase was deemed significant in Brown's website challenge.

PHILADELPHIA

In 1681, King Charles II of England paid off a debt to one of his admirals by offering his son and heir a block of land in North America. When I say a block, we are talking about an area the size of England! The offer was gladly accepted by William Penn, who was to make his land a home for the Quakers and other non-conforming religious groups. The land was named as 'Penn's woodland' – more familiar to us now as Pennsylvania.[132]

The capital of the state, Philadelphia, was to become the center of the American Revolution, with the Declaration of Independence being penned there. At the time of the Founding Fathers, Philadelphia was the largest city in the United States and also the 'second' capital while Washington, D.C. was being constructed.

Philadelphia may be used in *The Solomon Key* as it was, and still is, a center of the Masonic movement in the United States. Taken in conjunction with its relative proximity to Washington, D.C., it is possible that Dan Brown may use the city in his novel. The majestic setting of the Masonic Temple used by the Grand Lodge of Pennsylvania would certainly suit a Dan Brown novel, with its soaring cathedral-like exterior.

Fittingly, Philadelphia means 'brotherly love' in Greek.

UTOPIANS IN AMERICA

William Penn's 'land of tolerance' provided a safe haven for many religious groups which had been denounced by the Catholic and Protestant hierarchy. As such, it was seen as a kind of Utopia, free from the persecution found in Europe. Two of these Pennsylvanian groups in particular were quite influential.

The first was called the "Mystic Brotherhood", or "The Society of the Woman in the Wilderness" (sacred feminine fans stand up please). Founded by the respected mathematical scholar Johannes Kelpius, the group arrived in Philadelphia in 1694 and settled in the nearby countryside.

This society was highly respected by many Pennsylvanians due to their learned ways and skills in medicine. They were also talented musicians, and took great interest in numerology – the number 40 was of great importance to them, so we might add that number to our list of possible ciphers as well.

A second group which appeared after Kelpius' society was the 'Ephrata Cloister', which was founded by Johann Conrad Beissel at Ephrata in Lancaster County, Pennsylvania. The community was composed of celibate German pietists, who became well-known for their composition of hymns using four voices. However, the group may have had a more enduring legacy through their 'Utopian influence' on the ideas of some of the Founding Fathers. Both Benjamin Franklin and John Adams are known to have visited Ephrata and been impressed by the philosophy and wisdom of the group.[133]

There is little about these groups to suggest Dan Brown would make them a central part of *The Solomon Key*. However, considering their Utopian ideals and influence on the Founding Fathers, they may be mentioned in the narrative at some point. We have now come full circle in our investigation, and the Utopian ideal appears to be at the heart of the 'American experiment'. We will have to wait and see whether Brown makes it a theme of *The Solomon Key*.

CONCLUSION

AND NOW, WE WAIT...

This book is not meant as an encyclopedia of 'hidden history' themes to do with Freemasonry and the Founding Fathers of America. We have only covered each of them very superficially here, so I encourage the interested reader to seek out the original sources for more detailed information. For instance, David Ovason's research on the mysteries of Washington, D.C. in *The Secret Architecture of Our Nation's Capital,* is some five hundred pages in length – and only covers one of the many topics that we have rushed through in this book.

Instead, this book has simply been an exercise in fun, attempting to decode clues to the content of Dan Brown's *The Solomon Key* in advance, and provide a 'primer' on some of these subjects. We may well be wrong on a number of counts, and so it is hardly worth discussing in depth every possible option at Brown's disposal when composing his thriller. But I do hope that the information provided enables readers to digest *The Solomon Key* with a better understanding of the numerous topics involved.

There is no doubt that some of the subject matter we have covered will be in *The Solomon Key*. We know that Freemasonry is involved, and that the Founding Fathers and the architecture of Washington make appearances in the plot. The rest we have inferred, for better or for worse. Nonetheless, I think these subjects make for fascinating reading, whether Dan Brown includes them or not. However, there are a few questions regarding the composition of *The Solomon Key* which remain, and I pose them here for your own contemplation.

SECRET SOCIETY LOVE TRIANGLE

In *The Da Vinci Code*, Dan Brown often conflates three separate secret societies as being part of the one tradition: the Illuminati, the Priory of Sion, and the Freemasons. It will be interesting to see how he portrays Freemasonry in *The Solomon Key*, for a number of reasons.

In *Angels and Demons* the Illuminati are portrayed as an organization which, though perhaps entitled to their grievances, nevertheless could be quite vindictive in their actions. They also held science in much higher regard than religion. In *The Da Vinci Code* on the other hand, the Priory of Sion seem to be simply a bunch of genial individuals protecting a tremendous secret. Like the Illuminati, they do find themselves in opposition to the Catholic Church. However, in contrast to the secular Illuminati, they seem to be thoroughly based in goddess worship, the sacred bloodline of Jesus, and the mystical writings found beneath the Jerusalem Temple.

Freemasonry can be seen to have commonalities with both. The birth of the Royal Society, and the numerous inventors and scientists involved with the Craft, displays the links between Freemasonry, early science and the Enlightenment

– and by association, with Brown's version of the Illuminati. However, like the Priory of Sion, Masons also have many traditions involving secrets of the Jerusalem Temple, and the similar heritage involving the Knights Templar.

On the other hand, Freemasonry is often seen as quite a misogynistic organization – the ban upon female members (there are exceptions of course) seems in stark contrast to the 'sacred feminine' theme of the Priory of Sion in *The Da Vinci Code*. Nevertheless, there are references within the history of Freemasonry to some underlying goddess worship – be it through the Egyptian goddess Isis, the Christian Mary, Solomon's worship of Astarte, or the astrological Virgo. Perhaps Dan Brown will fall back on this evidence, as well as the similarities listed above, to connect the two organizations.

If, as it seems, the Great Seal is discussed regarding the Founding Fathers and Freemasonry, it will also be interesting to see how Brown handles this. For in *Angels and Demons* the Great Seal was discussed as an Illuminati device proclaiming their presence. This would suggest some sort of connection in Dan Brown's Langdon series between the Illuminati and Freemasonry – it will be fascinating to see if (and how) Brown creates this link.

In contemplating this information, the question begs asking: will Freemasonry be portrayed as 'good' or 'bad' in *The Solomon Key*? Considering that the Founding Fathers were involved in the Craft, it would be a tough sell for Brown to make them evil-doers. But he could fall back on making one branch of Masonry, or one of the Ivy League offshoots, to be dangerous renegades. Also, watch for the appearance of the Jesuits – their controversial history seems ready-made for a Robert Langdon thriller.

To Be Continued…

In considering whether Brown will make a link between the Priory of Sion and Freemasonry, it is worth asking if the novel will continue on immediately after the ending of *The Da Vinci Code*. Rosslyn Chapel certainly has connections with Freemasonry and pre-Columbus visits to America, and so it would provide a handy device for Brown to pivot the two plots upon. On the other hand though, it may seem a bit breathless for Langdon to jet back to the United States and continue on with another investigation on the back of the 'long night' of *The Da Vinci Code*.

The continuance question also raises other queries. Vittoria Vetra disappears after *Angels and Demons* with only the barest of mentions in the sequel – so what do we expect for Sophie's relationship with Robert Langdon? Considering she is part of Christ's bloodline, we would hope that she remains of some importance. And what of the chance that Langdon's old flame from *Angels and Demons* will reappear in the next offering, just to complicate things?

Was Langdon's search for the 'Holy Grail' completed in *The Da Vinci Code?* In that book, he mentions three parts to the legendary treasure: the bloodline of Christ, the body of the Magdalene, and the documents from under the Jerusalem Temple. Only the first two were notable in *The Da Vinci Code*, with the latter only mentioned in passing. Could it be that the plotline in Washington, D.C. will involve a treasure hunt involving these documents? The Kryptos quote provides a tantalizing clue that some sort of secret is hidden. Or perhaps a wildcard idea – something like the Ark of the Covenant, which Brown has not really mentioned, but does appear occasionally in much of the 'hidden history' that we have discussed.

Resources

I have mentioned my sources throughout this book, but it might be worthwhile to finish off by providing a list of books and websites which provide excellent in-depth reading on many of these topics. Here are my picks, in no particular order:

Books:

- *The Secret Architecture of Our Nation's Capital* – David Ovason
- *Talisman* – Graham Hancock and Robert Bauval
- *The Secret Teachings of All Ages* – Manly P. Hall
- *The Temple and the Lodge* – Michael Baigent and Richard Leigh
- *The Secret Destiny of America* – Manly P. Hall
- *The Rosicrucian Enlightenment* – Frances A. Yates
- *The Secret Symbols of the Dollar Bill* – David Ovason
- *Secrets of the Tomb* – Alexandra Robbins
- *Revolutionary Brotherhood* – Steven Bullock
- *The Code Book* – Simon Singh
- *The Freemasons* – Jasper Ridley
- *The Hiram Key* – Christopher Knight and Robert Lomas
- *The Second Messiah* – Christopher Knight and Robert Lomas
- *The Templar Revelation* – Lynn Picknett and Clive Prince
- *The Stargate Conspiracy* – Lynn Picknett and Clive Prince
- *Shadow of the Sentinel* – Bob Brewer and Warren Getler
- *The Da Vinci Code* – Dan Brown
- *Angels and Demons* – Dan Brown

Websites:

Dan Brown's official website, the center of all things Brownian. Resources for each of his books, links to breaking news, and home to the website challenges as well:

- http://www.danbrown.com/

The Web of Hiram website, an invaluable resource constructed by Robert Lomas on the history of Freemasonry. The website includes masses of historical documents concerning Freemasonry:

- http://www.bradford.ac.uk/webofhiram/

Albert Pike's *Morals and Dogma* online. Read Pike's rambling commentary on comparative religion and esoterica in full, rather than the short quotes often used out of context by anti-Masons:

- http://www.freemasons-freemasonry.com/apikefr.html

The website of the Grand Lodge of British Columbia and Yukon. Detailed essays on the history of Freemasonry, as well as sensible research into the various conspiracy theories regarding the Craft. Hours of great reading available:

- http://freemasonry.bcy.ca/GrandLodge.html

Website of the Supreme Council 33rd Degree, Scottish Rite Freemasonry, Southern Jurisdiction. Has numerous essays on Scottish Rite Masonry, as well as some beautiful photos of the 'House of the Temple' in Washington, D.C.:

- http://www.srmason-sj.org/web/

Website of the George Washington Masonic National Memorial. This website features the history behind the building, and provides an excellent tour of the Memorial with images of each room within.:

- http://www.gwmemorial.org/

Monticello, the home of Thomas Jefferson. Plenty of information about the third President of the United States, including information on his cipher systems:

- http://www.monticello.org/

The Kryptos homepage of Elonka Dunin. Everything there is to know about the enigmatic sculpture by James Sanborn – except for the final solution. Perhaps one day soon:

- http://elonka.com/kryptos/

Wikipedia, the free online community encyclopedia. Look out Britannica, there's a new kid in town:

- http://www.wikipedia.org/

Google's new map feature, which allows you to zoom right in on Washington, D.C. addresses – both in map form and via detailed satellite imagery. A great resource for surveying the design and monuments of the capital. You want detail? You can even see the step-pyramid which surmounts the Scottish Rite "House of the Temple"! You'll note though that the Capitol and White House are blurred out for security reasons:

- http://maps.google.com/

And don't forget to keep an eye on my very own website, The Daily Grail, which features daily news updates and essays on many of these topics:

- http://www.dailygrail.com/

APPENDIX

A VIEW OF THE CAPITAL

Readers not familiar with the layout of Washington, D.C. may have difficulty in visualizing some of the imagery discussed in this book. This appendix is thus aimed at allowing readers to better understand the relationships between various monuments and landmarks in the capital, through the presentation of a series of maps and views of the city.

Many of these images are historical, showing the gradual evolution of the layout and landmarks of Washington, D.C. Each one is presented as large as possible, and all are accompanied by a few comments to help the reader get their bearings. Hopefully when *The Solomon Key* is released, these will allow for a far better understanding of where Robert Langdon is at any one time.

Please note that while the maps are drawn to scale, some of the views do take some artistic licence and should not be trusted as exact representations. They do, however, allow a far better understanding of the city and so are presented here for the reader's benefit:

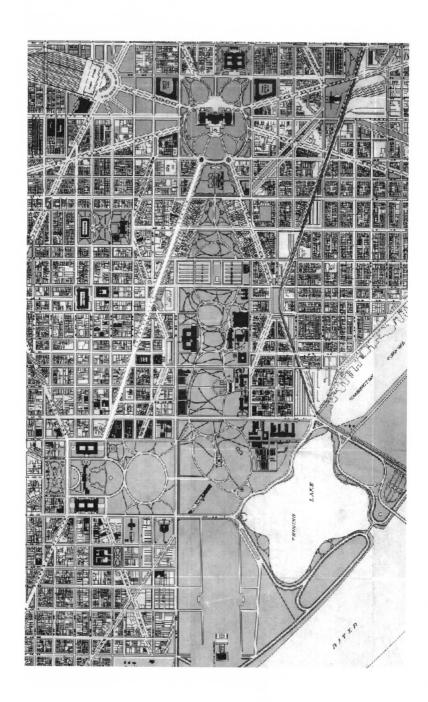

MAP OF WASHINGTON, D.C., 1918

This map shows the central part of Washington, D.C., which houses nearly all of the monuments noted in this book. North is to the left of the page, so it may be helpful to rotate the image clockwise by 90 degrees to get a more logical view of the map.

However, before rotating the page take a look at the 'Masonic Compass' design which can be seen more easily in this orientation. At the top of the page is the Capitol building, from which two 'legs' (and four 'arms') radiate: the left leg ends at the White House, while the right leg points at the future location of the Jefferson Memorial (construction began in 1939, 21 years after this map was created). Between these two points is the originally planned position of the Washington Monument, while the actual construction point is slightly higher up the page (to the east if looking at the page in its true orientation).

The Library of Congress sits at the very top of the page, directly to the east of the Capitol. The river in the picture is the Potomac.

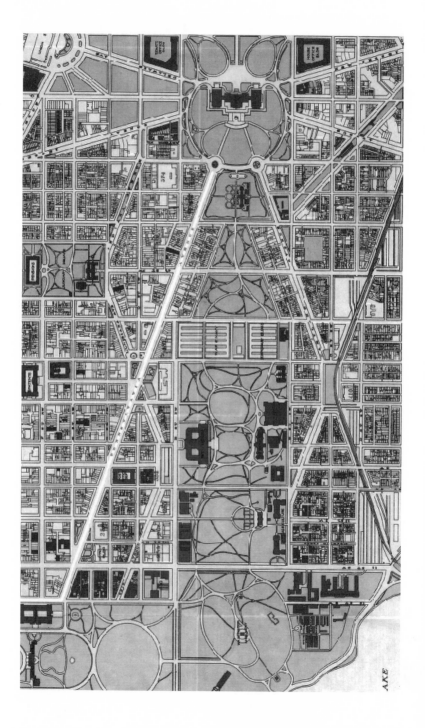

Map of Washington, D.C., 1918 (Detail)

This is the same map as on the previous page, although with more detail of the 'Federal Triangle'. This view shows more clearly how the Washington Monument no longer sits in true alignment with the planned position. The buildings 'above' the Washington Monument (to the east, remembering that north is to the left of the page) are the museums of the Smithsonian Institute.

This orientation also clearly shows the alleged 'owl' icon which is said by some conspiracy theorists to have been deliberately incorporated into the design of the Capitol. The owl is a motif of initation into the mysteries. At the top of the page, look for the eyes of the owl – the Capitol resides within its body, while the tail is flared out beneath the owl and is comprised mainly of the Botanic Gardens.

The left 'leg' leading between the Capitol and the White House is Pennsylvania Avenue. As mentioned in an earlier chapter, research has suggested that Pennsylvania Avenue is aligned with the rising of the star Sirius.

PLAN of the City of WASHINGTON.

Tiber Creek

Goose Creek

POTOMAK RIVER

EASTERN BRANCH

George Town

Lat. Capitol 38. 55. N.
Long. .... 0: O.

Original Map of Pierre l'Enfant, 1792

This map shows the original plan by Pierre l'Enfant, before any modifications took place. Note that the 'Federal Triangle', consisting of the planned locations of the White House, Capitol and the Washington Monument, is already in place. Similarly, the 'Masonic Compass' design using the Capitol as its mid-point is part of this design. However, numerous other aspects of the street layout were never implemented.

By tracing a line from the planned position of the Washington Monument, to the left (therefore north) through the White House, one can trace out the proposed 'Washington Meridian' mentioned in the book. The Scottish Rite 'House of the Temple' on 16th Street is found on this line, further to the north of the White House.

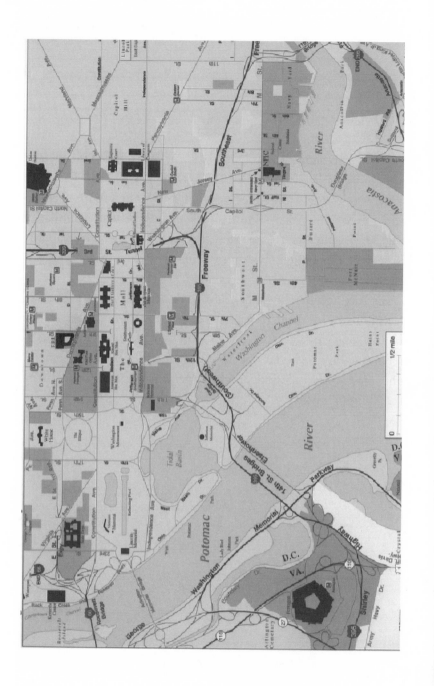

CURRENT STREET MAP OF WASHINGTON, D.C.

This simple map shows all the main features of the city – once again, north is to the left of the page. This view also shows the position of the Pentagon building at the bottom of the page, south-west across the Potomac River from the main part of Washington, D.C. The State Department can also be seen towards the bottom left corner of the page, west of the White House, while the Lincoln Memorial lies to the west of the Washington Monument. The alignment between the White House and the Jefferson Memorial can also be seen quite clearly in this image.

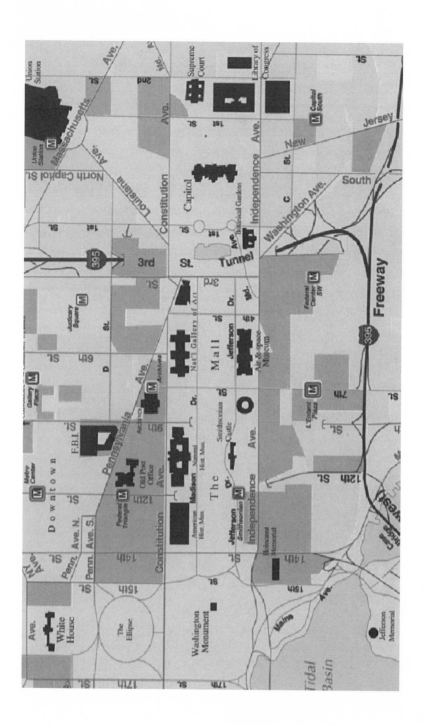

CURRENT STREET MAP (DETAIL)

Zooming in on the previous map gives more detail to the Federal Triangle, as well as showing Union Station in the top-left corner. The F.B.I. building can be seen on Pennsylvania Avenue. To the east of the F.B.I. building is Judiciary Square, where the controversial statue of Albert Pike resides.

The offset of the Washington Monument from the 'meridian' running through the White House and Jefferson Memorial is quite evident. Within the Federal Triangle can be found the National Gallery of Art as well as the Air and Space Museum (just to the west of the Capitol). Closer to the Washington Monument are the main Smithsonian building ('The Castle'), the American History Museum and the Natural History Museum. The National Archives borders Pennsylvania Avenue.

Above the Capitol (to the east) is the Library of Congress and the Supreme Court.

Birds-Eye View Looking North-West

This birds-eye view from behind the Capitol building, and looking north-west, shows both the 'Masonic Compass' and the Federal Triangle quite clearly. Union Station is at the top of the page, not far from the Capitol Building. Readers may find it useful to cross-reference between this view and the previous map as this early representation is missing a number of landmarks.

Birds-Eye View Looking North-East

This birds-eye view from almost above the site of the Pentagon building is dated 1916, and shows the limited development of the city even in the 20th Century. The impressive site of the Capitol Building, on Jenkins Hill, is evident in this image. Neither the Jefferson Memorial nor the Pentagon were constructed at the time this image was commissioned – in fact, it would be another two decades before construction of the Jefferson Memorial was undertaken.

ENDNOTES

[1] *The Decipherment of Linear B*, John Chadwick, cited in *The Code Book*, Simon Singh

[2] http://www.randomhouse.com/doubleday/davinci

[3] http://www.nytimes.com/2004/10/28/books/28brow.html

[4] http://www.danbrown.com/novels/davinci_code/faqs.html

[5] http://www.bookbrowse.com/index.cfm?page=author&authorID=226&view=interview

[6] http://www.artsjournal.com/man/archives20040201.shtml

[7] http://www.egyptianmyths.net/udjat.htm

[8] Wikipedia, http://en.wikipedia.org/wiki/Angels_and_Demons (Ahsirakh)

[9] http://www.bookbrowse.com/index.cfm?page=author&authorID=226&view=interview

[10] *The Rosicrucian Enlightenment*, Frances A. Yates

[11] "The Rosicrucian Dream", Christopher McIntosh, in *The Inner West*, ed. Jay Kinney

[12] *The Rosicrucian Enlightenment*, Frances A. Yates

[13] Ibid.

[14] Ibid.

[15] *The Way of Light*, John Amos Comenius, trans. E.T. Campagnac

[16] *The Rosicrucian Enlightenment*, Frances A. Yates

[17] King James Bible, I Kings V: 3-5

[18] King James Bible, I Kings VII: 13-21

[19] *The Temple and the Lodge,* Michael Baigent and Richard Leigh

[20] Ibid.

[21] Cited in "The Hidden Sages and the Knights Templar", Robert Richardson, in *The Inner West,* ed. Jay Kinney

[22] 'Oration', Andrew Michael Ramsay

[23] Ibid.

[24] Ibid.

[25] *Digging Up Jerusalem,* K.M.Kenyon, cited in *The Second Messiah,* Robert Lomas and Christopher Knight

[26] *Holy Blood, Holy Grail,* Michael Baigent, Richard Leigh, Henry Lincoln

[27] Ibid.

[28] "The Knights Templar in Scotland", R. Aitken, cited in *The Temple and the Lodge,* Michael Baigent and Richard Leigh

[29] *The Second Messiah,* Robert Lomas and Christopher Knight

[30] *The Hiram Key,* Robert Lomas and Christopher Knight

[31] *The Second Messiah,* Robert Lomas and Christopher Knight

[32] *An Encyclopedia of Occultism,* Lewis Spence, cited in *The Templar Revelation,* Lynn Picknett and Clive Prince

[33] *The Temple and the Lodge,* Michael Baigent and Richard Leigh

[34] *Book of Constitutions,* Rev. James Anderson

[35] *Early Masonic Pamphlets,* Knoop, Jones and Hamer, cited in *The Rosicrucian Enlightenment,* Frances A. Yates

[36] "Historico-Critical Inquiry into the Origins of the Rosicrucians and the Freemasons", Thomas de Quincey, cited in *The Rosicrucian Enlightenment,* Frances A. Yates

[37] *The Rosicrucian Enlightenment,* Frances A. Yates

[38] *The Secret Lore of Egypt: Its Impact on the West,* Erik Hornung, trans. David Lorton

[39] *The Secret Symbols of the Dollar Bill,* David Ovason

[40] *The Temple and the Lodge,* Michael Baigent and Richard Leigh

[41] *The Secret Destiny of America,* Manly P. Hall

⁴² *The Temple and the Lodge*, Michael Baigent and Richard Leigh

⁴³ Ibid.

⁴⁴ Ibid.

⁴⁵ *Talisman*, Robert Bauval and Graham Hancock

⁴⁶ Ibid.

⁴⁷ Wikipedia, http://en.wikipedia.org/wiki/Thomas_jefferson

⁴⁸ http://freemasonry.bcy.ca/anti-masonry/jefferson.html

⁴⁹ Wikipedia, http://en.wikipedia.org/wiki/Thomas_Paine

⁵⁰ Ibid.

⁵¹ *Age of Reason*, Thomas Paine

⁵² "The Origins of Freemasonry", Thomas Paine

⁵³ Ibid.

⁵⁴ *Talisman*, Robert Bauval and Graham Hancock

⁵⁵ "The Origins of Freemasonry", Thomas Paine

⁵⁶ *The Diary and Sundry Observations*, ed. Dagobert D. Runes

⁵⁷ *Talisman*, Robert Bauval and Graham Hancock

⁵⁸ Ibid.

⁵⁹ Wikipedia, http://en.wikipedia.org/wiki/Haym_Solomon

⁶⁰ *The Secret Destiny of America*, Manly P. Hall

⁶¹ Ibid.

⁶² Ibid.

⁶³ *Talisman*, Robert Bauval and Graham Hancock

⁶⁴ Cited in *The Temple and the Lodge*, Michael Baigent and Richard Leigh

⁶⁵ http://www.indystar.com/articles/2/190395-5902-047.html

⁶⁶ *The Secret Architecture of Our Nation's Capital*, David Ovason

⁶⁷ *Talisman*, Robert Bauval and Graham Hancock

⁶⁸ http://freemasonry.bcy.ca/anti-masonry/washington_dc/ovason.html

⁶⁹ *The Secret Architecture of Our Nation's Capital*, David Ovason

⁷⁰ *Talisman*, Robert Bauval and Graham Hancock

⁷¹ Ibid.

⁷² http://www.nps.gov/wamo/history/chap2.htm

⁷³ http://www.nps.gov/wamo/history/chap1.htm

⁷⁴ *Talisman*, Robert Bauval and Graham Hancock

[75] *The Secret Architecture of Our Nation's Capital*, David Ovason

[76] http://www.fiu.edu/~mizrachs/poseur3.html

[77] http://www.cr.nps.gov/nr/travel/wash/dc48.htm

[78] *Talisman*, Robert Bauval and Graham Hancock

[79] *The Great Seal of the United States*, US Department of State

[80] Ibid.

[81] Ibid.

[82] *The Secret Teachings of All Ages*, Manly P. Hall

[83] *The Secret Symbols of the Dollar Bill*, David Ovason

[84] Ibid.

[85] Cited in *America's Secret Destiny*, Robert Hieronimus,

[86] *The Secret Symbols of the Dollar Bill*, David Ovason

[87] *The Secret Architecture of Our Nation's Capital*, David Ovason

[88] *Early Masonic Pamphlets*, ed. D. Knoop, G.P. Jones and D. Hamer

[89] *Talisman*, Robert Bauval and Graham Hancock

[90] "Two Sides But Only One Die: The Great Seal of the United States", M. L. Lien, cited in *Talisman*, Robert Bauval and Graham Hancock

[91] *The Secret Symbols of the Dollar Bill*, David Ovason

[92] *Talisman*, Robert Bauval and Graham Hancock

[93] *The Stargate Conspiracy*, Lynn Picknett and Clive Prince

[94] Ibid.

[95] Edgar Cayce, reading 1152-11, cited in *Secret Chamber*, Robert Bauval

[96] "Changing Images of Man", Willis W. Harman, cited in *The Stargate Conspiracy*, Lynn Picknett and Clive Prince

[97] Cited in *Holy Blood, Holy Grail*, Michael Baigent, Richard Leigh and Henry Lincoln

[98] http://www.msnbc.msn.com/id/4179618/

[99] http://msnbc.msn.com/id/3080246/

[100] *Secrets of the Tomb*, Alexandra Robbins

[101] Ron Rosenbaum, cited in *Secrets of the Tomb*, Alexandra Robbins

[102] http://freemasonry.bcy.ca/anti-masonry/anti-masonry05.html

[103] *The Da Vinci Code*, Dan Brown

[104] *The Secret Teachings of All Ages*, Manly P. Hall

[105] Ibid.

[106] Ibid.

[107] Ibid.

[108] http://www.fbrt.org.uk/pages/essays/essay-ciphers.html

[109] *Modern Magick*, Donald Michael Kraig

[110] Ibid.

[111] Ibid.

[112] *The Key of Solomon*, S. Liddell Macgregor Mathers

[113] http://www.danbrown.com

[114] http://www.monticello.org/reports/interests/wheel_cipher.html

[115] http://www.ideosphere.com/fx/lists/fx-discuss/1999/0930.html

[116] http://elonka.com/kryptos/faq.html

[117] Cited in *Talisman*, Robert Bauval and Graham Hancock

[118] *The Zelator*, Mark Hedsel and David Ovason

[119] *The Second Messiah*, Christopher Knight and Robert Lomas

[120] http://www.geocities.com/nu_isis/fonts.html

[121] http://www.reformation.org/oath.html

[122] Ibid.

[123] Ibid.

[124] http://www.thehill.com/under_dome/110404.aspx

[125] Letter from Adams to Thomas Jefferson, May 5th 1816

[126] Wikipedia, http://en.wikipedia.org/wiki/Oak_Island

[127] "The Secrets of Oak Island", Joe Nickell, in *Skeptical Inquirer 24:2*

[128] Wikipedia, http://en.wikipedia.org/wiki/Oak_Island

[129] *Shadow of the Sentinel*, Bob Brewer and Warren Getler

[130] *The New Freedom*, Woodrow Wilson

[131] Wikipedia, http://en.wikipedia.org/wiki/Joseph_Smith

[132] *Talisman*, Robert Bauval and Graham Hancock

[133] http://www.fiu.edu/~mizrachs/utopo-amer.html

INDEX